The Power of Concentration

The Power of Concentration

Theron Q. Dumont

DD BOOKS
Publishers for New Generations

First Published: 2024

Book Name: The Power of Concentration (Illustrated)
Author: William Walker Atkinson

Illustrated by **DD Books**

Price (INR): 250/-
ISBN: 978-93-5957-888-0
Published by **DD BOOKS**
Email: **ddsalesglobal@gmail.com**

Table of content

Introduction

We all understand the necessity of concentration to achieve our goals. Learning how to concentrate is invaluable. To succeed in any endeavor, you must be able to focus your entire mind on the task at hand.

Don't be disheartened if you struggle to maintain your focus initially; few can do so effortlessly. Interestingly, it often seems easier to concentrate on things that aren't beneficial for us rather than those that are. However, this tendency can be overcome through conscious effort.

By practicing concentration exercises daily, you'll soon develop this essential skill. Success becomes attainable when you can concentrate, allowing you to harness constructive thoughts while blocking out destructive ones. It's crucial to think only thoughts that will benefit you.

Have you ever considered the significant role your concentrated thoughts play in your life? This book explores their profound and enduring effects.

The lessons presented here are highly practical, and the exercises have been thoroughly tested. They are structured to show improvement from the outset, providing encouragement and demonstrating ways to self-improve.

Human potential is immense, but it must be cultivated and refined to be useful. Every individual can achieve great things when awakened to their full potential. However, even the most talented individual will achieve little without concentration and effort. A focused mind can accomplish more than mere talent; it's the ability to concentrate on every possibility that elevates both work and life.

True advancement stems from individual effort. These lessons will inspire and motivate you toward success, aligning you with the principles of achievement and giving you a stronger grasp on your duties and responsibilities.

The methods of thought concentration outlined in this work, when put into practice, will unlock inner pathways connecting you with the eternal laws of existence and their infinite wellspring of unchanging truth.

Since people are diverse, it's impossible to provide instructions equally beneficial to all. The author has aimed to awaken and nurture that inner aspect which words alone may not fully express. Therefore, study these lessons as a means of awakening and cultivating what lies within you. Let all your actions and thoughts possess the intensity and power of concentration.

To fully benefit from these lessons, read a page, then close the book and reflect on its ideas. Doing so will cultivate a habit of concentrated thought, enabling you to read quickly and remember all that you read.

☸☸☸

Lesson 1

Concentration Finds the Way

Everyone possesses two natures. One urges us to progress, while the other seeks to hold us back. The nature we nurture and focus on determines our ultimate character. Both aspects vie for dominance, yet it's the will alone that determines the outcome. With one decisive act of will, a person can alter their entire trajectory and achieve nearly miraculous feats. You could be that person. You have the potential if you truly desire it, for the will can uncover a path or forge one.

I could recount numerous cases where individuals, seemingly trudging along in a routine manner, suddenly awakened as if from a slumber, realizing the latent potential within them. From that moment forward, they were transformed beings. You alone determine when this pivotal moment occurs. It's a matter of choice whether we allow our higher self to guide us or succumb to the baser instincts within. No one is compelled to do anything against their will. Thus, each person is the architect of their own destiny if they so will it. Our actions are a product of our conditioning. We are malleable, shaped entirely by the power of our will.

Habit is something acquired. You often hear people say, "He takes after his parents; it runs in the family," implying that a person is simply following in their parents' footsteps. While this may frequently be the case, there's no inherent reason for it, as a person can break a habit the moment they master the determination to do so. A man may have been deemed worthless all his life until this very moment, yet from here on, he can begin to make something of himself. Even in old age, individuals have experienced sudden transformations and achieved remarkable feats. "I missed my chance," one might lament. While that may be true, sheer force of will can create another opportunity for us. There's no truth to the notion that opportunity knocks only once in a lifetime. In reality, opportunity never seeks us out; it's we who must seek it. What may appear as one person's opportunity was another's loss. In today's world, one person's intellect is pitted against another's. Often, it's the swiftness of action that determines the outcome. One person thinks, "I'll do it," but while they procrastinate, another takes action and completes the task. Both had the same opportunity. The one who hesitates may bemoan their missed chance, but it should serve as a lesson, guiding them toward the path of success.

Many individuals read fine literature but claim to derive little benefit from it. They fail to grasp that the purpose of any book or course is merely to awaken them to their potential and spur them to exercise their willpower. You can instruct a person endlessly, yet they will only truly learn what they discover for themselves. "You can lead a horse to water, but you can't make it drink."

One of the most rewarding practices I know of is that of seeking the good in everyone and everything, for goodness exists in all things. By recognizing a person's positive qualities, we uplift and encourage them, and in turn, benefit ourselves. We earn their goodwill, a precious asset at times. We receive what we give. There comes a time when most of us need encouragement, need lifting up. Therefore, cultivate the habit of uplifting others, and you will find it to be a marvelous tonic for both those you encourage and yourself, as you receive encouraging and uplifting thoughts in return.

Life offers us opportunities for improvement, but whether we seize them depends on how closely we adhere to expectations. At the beginning of each month, one should reflect on their progress. If they haven't met expectations, they must identify the reasons and strive to surpass them through additional effort. Every time we fall short of our goals, we lose that time irretrievably. While we may find excuses, most are poor substitutes for action. Most things are within reach. Though our tasks may be arduous, the greater the challenge, the greater the reward. It's the difficult tasks that truly shape us; endeavors requiring minimal effort utilize few of our faculties and yield scant achievements. Therefore, do not shy away from challenges, for accomplishing them often brings greater benefits than numerous smaller triumphs.

I firmly believe that any person willing to pay the price can achieve success. The price isn't monetary but rather effort. The primary quality essential for success is the desire to act—to become something. Next is learning how to act, then implementing that knowledge. The most effective individuals possess broad minds, having acquired knowledge that, while perhaps unrelated to a specific situation, holds value across various contexts. Thus, those striving for success must be open-minded and seek knowledge in all areas of their field. Such individuals attain success.

The secret to success lies in continually striving for self-improvement, regardless of one's circumstances or position. Learn all that you can. Don't aim to do the minimum but rather the maximum. Such individuals are always in demand, earning reputations as industrious workers. Progressive companies seldom let such individuals leave their employ if they can help it.

Those who reach the pinnacle are hardworking, determined individuals, not timid or slow workers. Untried individuals rarely assume positions of responsibility and authority. Those selected have demonstrated their capabilities, achieved results, or taken initiative in their respective domains. They are chosen for their reputation for injecting vigor and determination into their efforts.

The individual selected in crucial moments is typically not a genius; they possess no more talent than others. However, they understand that results stem from unwavering, concentrated effort. Miracles in business don't simply occur; they're the product of persistence and determination. This is the secret to why some succeed while others fail. Successful individuals become accustomed to achieving goals and consistently anticipate success. Conversely, those who fail become accustomed to failure, expecting it and drawing it towards themselves.

In my opinion, with proper training, every individual could achieve success. It's regrettable that so many talented individuals are allowed to go to waste. Someday, I hope to see a philanthropist establish a school to train those who have faltered. Practical psychology could work wonders in a year's time. Agencies could be established to identify individuals who have lost their way, providing them with the support needed to regain their footing. Often, they merely need a push to realize their latent potential. It's my hope that someone will seize this opportunity to guide those who have begun to falter toward success.

Today, when a person loses their way, they must reclaim their redemption through their own willpower. They will receive little encouragement or inspiring advice. They must find their way back alone, abandoning dissipative behaviors and focusing on building a meaningful career. Today, we must overcome our weaknesses independently. Don't expect others to assist you. Summon your resolve, make firm resolutions, and commit to conquering your weaknesses and vices. Ultimately, only you can achieve this. Others can encourage you, but that's all.

There's nothing, except for health, that should hinder someone from achieving success. No other obstacle cannot be overcome. To surmount a handicap, one must simply exhibit more determination, grit, and willpower.

A person with determination and willpower may be impoverished today and wealthy in a few years. Willpower is a more valuable asset than money; it can carry you over the chasms of failure if given the chance.

Those who have risen to the highest positions have often overcome substantial odds. Consider the hardships endured by many inventors before achieving success. They were frequently misunderstood by relatives and friends and often lacked life's basic necessities. Yet, through sheer determination and courage, they persisted until perfecting their inventions, which ultimately improved the lives of others.

Everyone desires to achieve something, but few are willing to exert the necessary effort or make the required sacrifices. There's only one way to accomplish anything: take action. Nearly anything can be achieved today if one sets their heart on it and allows nothing to hinder their progress. Obstacles are swiftly overcome by those determined to fulfill their aspirations. The bigger the individual, the smaller the obstacle appears. Always focus on the advantage gained by overcoming obstacles; it will provide the courage needed for their conquest.

Do not anticipate smooth sailing at all times. Certain segments of your journey are bound to be rough. However, don't allow these rough patches to deter you. Keep moving forward on your journey. How you navigate through the storms reveals your resilience. Instead of dwelling on the rough spots, reminisce about the pleasant stretches you've already traversed. Look ahead with optimism at the smooth plains awaiting you.

Do not allow setbacks to halt your progress. Regard them as temporary obstacles that must be overcome on your path to achieving your goals.

☸☸☸

Lesson 2

The Self-mastery: Self-direction Power of Concentration

From a psychological standpoint, man often falls short of what he could be. He lacks the self-mastery, the ability to direct his focus and concentration, which rightfully belongs to him. This deficiency arises from a lack of training in promoting self-mastery. Every well-balanced mind possesses faculties whose primary function is to organize, direct, and concentrate the operations of the mind, both mentally and physically. Man must learn to control not only his thoughts but also his physical movements.

When these controlling faculties are underdeveloped, impulses, emotions, thoughts, actions, and habits lack regulation, resulting in poor mental concentration. This isn't due to inherent weakness in the faculties themselves but rather to a lack of proper training. Without well-developed self-regulating faculties, impulses, appetites, emotions, and passions have free rein, leading to impulsivity, restlessness, emotional volatility, and irregularity in mental functioning. Consequently, mental concentration suffers.

To develop concentration, one must first cultivate the necessary powers that enable concentration. Therefore, if one struggles to concentrate, it could be due to one of the following reasons:

1. Deficiency of the motor centers.

2. An impulsive and emotional mindset.
3. Lack of training.

The last issue can be readily rectified through systematic practice, as it's the easiest to correct. Overcoming an impulsive and emotional state of mind requires restraining anger, passion, excitement, hatred, and other intense emotions. It's impossible to concentrate effectively when in such heightened emotional states.

These tendencies can be diminished by avoiding foods and drinks that weaken or stimulate the nerves or incite passions and emotions. Associating with steady, calm, controlled, and conservative individuals can also be beneficial.

Addressing deficiencies in the motor centers is more challenging, as it requires developing willpower. This process takes time, but those afflicted may benefit from reading and studying courses such as "The Master Mind."

Many mistakenly believe that being in a negative state equates to concentration, but this is not the case. Individuals in a negative state often experience abstraction of the mind or absentmindedness rather than true concentration. Prolonged periods of negativity can weaken concentration and even harm the brain. Concentration requires mental strength; individuals lacking strength of mind cannot effectively concentrate. Weak minds struggle to focus on specific subjects or thoughts and find it difficult to shift their focus when needed. Conversely, those with strength of mind can center their thoughts on any problem and remove any disharmonious impressions. Concentration, fundamentally, signifies strength of mind.

Through concentration, one can harness and direct their mental and physical energies. A concentrated mind pays close attention to thoughts, words, actions, and plans. Individuals who allow their minds to wander aimlessly will struggle to accomplish much in life, as they squander their energies. Aimless work, thought, speech, and action, coupled with a wandering mind, hinder concentration. True concentration occurs when one declares, "I want to, I can, I will."

Some common mistakes individuals make include wasting time reading sensational stories or worthless newspaper articles, which excite impulsive and emotional faculties, thereby weakening concentration. Concentration can only be developed through close self-observation. All forms of development begin with attentive observation. Regulate every thought and feeling, watch your own actions and those of others, and gradually improve your self-control until you can engineer every thought, wish, and plan. Focusing the mind consciously on the task at hand leads to concentration. Only a trained mind can focus. Concentration involves holding a thought before the mind until all faculties have thoroughly considered it.

Individuals unable to direct their thoughts, wishes, plans, resolutions, and studies cannot achieve their full potential. Those who fluctuate between impulsivity and calm lack proper self-control and cannot master their minds, thoughts, feelings, or wishes. Such individuals cannot achieve success. Irritability impedes their progress and disrupts the efforts of those around them. In contrast, those who can direct their energies and maintain concentration control their actions, directing each movement toward a useful end and every thought toward a noble purpose.

In modern society, individuals who become agitated and irritable are viewed unfavorably. Those with good manners speak deliberately and cultivate an increasingly composed demeanor. They remain consciously attentive, focusing their minds on one thing at a time and shutting out distractions. When conversing with others, give them your undivided attention. Do not allow your focus to waver or be diverted. Coordinate your will and intellect to act in harmony.

Challenge yourself to maintain self-possession throughout the day. Periodically assess your actions to ensure you've stayed true to your determination. The more self-possessed you are, the better your concentration will be. Avoid rushing, and remember that improving your concentration increases your potential for success. Concentration leads to success because it enhances self-governance and mental focus, intensifies your commitment to your pursuits, and consequently improves your chances of success.

When engaging in conversation with someone, maintain focus on your own plans and objectives. Concentrate your strength on the purpose you are discussing. Watch the other person's every move, but keep your own plans in mind. Failing to do so will result in wasted energy and a lack of accomplishment.

Observe individuals known for their strong character and forcefulness. Notice their perfect control over their bodies. Then, observe an ordinary person and notice the unnecessary expenditure of energy in their eye movements, arm movements, and finger movements. These movements break down vital cells and diminish the person's power in vital and nerve directions. Conserving nervous forces is as crucial as conserving vital forces.

Excitement quickly depletes nerve force, rendering an irritable person less magnetic and admired. Anger, sarcasm, and excitement weaken individuals in this regard. Those who allow themselves to become excited will eventually become nervous due to the depletion of nerve forces and vital energies. Such individuals struggle to concentrate.

When the mind can concentrate properly, the energy of every microscopic cell is directed into one channel, resulting in a powerful personal influence. Each person possesses millions of tiny trembling cells, each with a center where life and energy are stored and generated. When this energy is conserved and controlled, the person is influential; otherwise, they are not influential or successful.

Just as a steam engine cannot run with all its valves open, wasting energy prevents individuals from performing at their best. Each neuron in the brain's gray layers serves as a psychic center of thought and action, pulsating with intelligent force. When this force, thoughts, and motions are controlled by a conservative, systematic, and concentrated mind, the result is magnetism, vitality, and health. The muscles, bones, ligaments, hands, feet, and nerves serve as agents for carrying out the mind's mandates. The volitional faculties' sole purpose is to move the physical mechanism as energy travels along the nerves and muscles. By exerting voluntary control over these messages, impulses, thoughts, emotions, and physical movements, individuals develop self-mastery and enhance their power of concentration in proportion.

Any activity or task that stimulates the mind, activates the senses, arouses emotions and appetites, causes confusion, fear, or emotional turmoil, weakens concentration. This is why all forms of excitement are detrimental. Individuals who consume strong drinks, indulge in fits of temper, engage in fights, consume stimulating food, sing and dance excessively, thus arousing their emotions, or exhibit sudden, vehement, and emotional behavior, lack the ability to concentrate. Conversely, those whose actions are slower and guided by intelligence develop concentration. Occasionally, dogmatic, willful, excitable individuals can concentrate, but their concentration is spasmodic and erratic rather than controlled and consistent. Their energy fluctuates; sometimes abundant, other times scarce; easily provoked and easily wasted. An analogy to understand this is likening it to the discharge of a gun. If the gun fires when intended, it serves its purpose, but if it fires prematurely, it not only wastes ammunition but may also cause damage. Similarly, many individuals allow their energy to explode, wasting it and endangering others, thereby squandering their power and magnetism, and compromising their chances of success. Such individuals are generally not well-liked and will struggle to gain favor until they gain control over themselves.

To overcome these challenges, individuals need to practice various concentration exercises consistently over time. They must eliminate sudden, erratic thoughts, regulate their emotions and movements, and train their minds to remain steady and focused throughout the day.

The lower area of the brain serves as the reservoir of energy. Most individuals possess all the dynamic energy they need, provided they can concentrate it. However, they must also develop the skills to regulate and direct this energy effectively. Without these engineering qualities, individuals will struggle to achieve much in life. A good engineer controls every action, and all work contributes to development. Every action either propels one forward or leads to deterioration, a principle worth remembering when deciding whether to engage in an activity.

I firmly believe in the principle of "work when you work, and play when you play." By fully immersing oneself in pleasure or love, one can develop concentration. Similarly, focusing on the "self" and its potential leads to enhanced concentration and self-esteem. Systematically concentrating on tasks leads to increased power, as systematic action requires concentration. Even seemingly mundane activities, such as walking in nature, observing vegetation, or maintaining punctuality, contribute to concentration development. However, inconsistent habits hinder concentration, whereas fixing one's mind on a specific thought at successive intervals fosters concentration.

If you focus your mind on a chosen object, you concentrate your attention, similar to how a camera lens focuses on a specific landscape. Therefore, always maintain your focus on whatever task you are performing, regardless of its nature. Keep a vigilant watch over yourself, as without doing so, your progress will be slow.

Practicing deep, prolonged breaths is not only beneficial for health improvement, although that is significant, but also for the purpose of cultivating more power, love, and vitality. All activities contribute to development.

While you may find it peculiar to develop concentration through muscular exercises, it's essential to remember that the mind is closely linked with muscles and nerves. When you stabilize your nerves and muscles, you also stabilize your mind. Conversely, if your nerves become unsettled, your mind becomes erratic, and you lose the power of direction, which is concentration. Therefore, exercises that steady the nerves and muscles are crucial for concentration development.

Everyone continuously receives impulses that require direction and control for a successful life. This is why it's important to control the movements of the eyes, feet, fingers, etc. It's also why controlling breathing is essential. Slow, deep exhalations are incredibly valuable as they stabilize circulation, heart action, muscles, and nerves, leading to a steady mind. Irregular heartbeats and uneven lung action result in an unsteady mind unsuitable for concentration. Hence, controlled breathing is foundational for physical health.

You must not only concentrate your mind but also the actions of your eyes, ears, and fingers. Each of these contains miniature minds controlled by the master engineer. Understanding this concept thoroughly accelerates your development.

Observing prominent individuals or reading their biographies reveals that they often let others do the talking. It's much easier to talk than to listen.

There is no better exercise for concentration than paying close attention when someone is speaking. In addition to learning from their words, you can enhance both mental and physical concentration.

When you shake hands with someone, think of your hand as containing hundreds of individual minds, each with their own intelligence. This can add personality to your handshake. A listless handshake shows timidity, lack of force, and a weak personality. On the other hand, a strong and passionate handshake reflects a developed soul and strong magnetism. When two individuals with strong personalities shake hands, they feel a thrill as their energies meet. Love arouses positive and negative energies, while its absence can make life dull.

To master the art of handshaking and social affection, observe how you breathe in different situations. When you're happy, your breathing is plentiful and oxygen-rich, filling your soul with love. This love develops you physically, mentally, and socially. Breathe deeply when you're happy to gain strength and concentration.

To get more out of life, focus on love and affection. This will add sweetness, magnetism, and sentiment to your life. To concentrate love in your handshake, ensure it is steady and controlled. When you feel irritable, use your will to practice patience, breathe slowly and deeply, and speak clearly. This exercise in self-control will improve your concentration and overall demeanor.

When meeting significant people, maintain a relaxed and composed attitude. Observe both them and yourself. Static exercises, like standing tall with a straight posture and deep breathing, help develop motor skills and improve concentration. If you feel irritable or nervous, this posture can help calm you down.

Avoid spending time with irritable or negative people until you strengthen your concentration abilities. Engaging in exercises that enhance control over body parts like ears, fingers, and eyes can help steady your mind. A steady gaze, for example, indicates a steady mind.

Studying a person's actions can reveal their mental state, as actions are a reflection of the mind. A composed mind leads to composed actions. Concentration requires control over both mind and body, as they are interconnected.

Some people may seem unambitious due to sluggish minds, but they often have good control. However, they lack energy and force, which limits their potential. To improve, one must develop mental and physical energy and learn to direct and hold it at a point.

Physical culture benefits are often overlooked, but static exercises are particularly effective in maintaining sustained control over faculties. By mastering control over the body, you can also gain control over the mind.

Lesson 3

How to Gain what You Want through Concentration

Some people may question the power of concentration, saying that merely desiring something won't make it happen. However, through focused concentration, you can achieve your goals and fulfill your desires. Wishing for something without taking action demonstrates weakness and disbelief. Instead, create a mental image of what you want and concentrate on making it a reality.

Never allow yourself to drift aimlessly. Know what you want and strive relentlessly to achieve it. As an example, when someone wants to obtain a specific item, they persistently seek information until they find a way to get it. This determination is the secret to successful concentration.

Your soul holds immense power, and you can accomplish anything you set your mind to. The phrase "I'll find a way or make one!" embodies this winning spirit. One man, who eventually became the head of a large bank, started as a messenger boy. His father encouraged him to concentrate on becoming the president by wearing a button with a secret message. Each day, his father asked what he had done to progress towards his goal. This constant reminder helped him concentrate on his ambition, and he eventually achieved it.

Don't waste your mental energy on idle wishes or pursuing every whim. Instead, focus on meaningful goals and put in the necessary effort to succeed. Emerson said, "Power to him who power exerts." Success today depends on tapping into your inner force, which, when applied in your endeavors, ensures lasting results.

To reach your full potential, you must learn to concentrate on the Interior law of force. By doing so, you awaken your thought powers, which, when applied in your work, lead to lasting achievements. As long as you are willing to put in the effort, you can accomplish anything right and just.

Believe in your abilities and your capacity to overcome challenges. You possess the latent faculties and forces needed to overcome obstacles and achieve your goals. Embrace the unconquerable law within you, and let it empower you to face life's difficulties.

Remain determined and focused on your objectives, knowing that you represent the infinite law of force. Your inner strength will help you conquer any obstacle that stands in your way. Trust in your abilities and the righteousness of your cause, and you will find success.

Lesson 4

Concentration - The Quiet Force that Creates Outcomes in all Business

First, understand the immense power thoughts hold. A single fearful thought can cause physical harm, like turning someone's hair gray overnight. In another example, a condemned prisoner, believing he was losing blood, died from mental fear even though the situation wasn't life-threatening. These instances demonstrate the significant impact thoughts have on our lives.

Learning the power of concentration is crucial for personal growth. You're constantly surrounded by various thoughts, some good and others not so good. To avoid absorbing negative influences, cultivate a positive mental attitude.

Studying unneeded moods like anxiety, worry, despondency, and discouragement, which stem from uncontrolled thoughts, will help you appreciate the importance of thought control. Your thoughts shape who you are, just like a mirror reflects your appearance. Observing people's faces on the street can reveal their life experiences and choices.

Mastering thought power can unlock hidden potential within you. Remember, your thoughts create your environment, friends, and circumstances. Positive thoughts build, while negative thoughts tear down. A strong desire to do what's right carries immense power.

Understand the value of your thoughts and how they influence you through invisible connections. If your thoughts are positive, you'll attract like-minded individuals and gain their trust. As your thoughts evolve, so will your surroundings. This is a practical lesson to learn. Good thoughts foster growth, while evil thoughts hinder. The power to do right is immense.

Recognize the impact of your thoughts on your life and learn to harness their power to create a positive and successful environment for yourself.

Thoughts of Right and Good Will bring you into harmony with successful people who can help you when needed. Understanding the power of concentration is vital for personal growth and gaining others' trust.

When you meet someone, their attitude influences your instincts. Trustworthy people inspire confidence. Be mindful of your thoughts, as they shape your life and actions. Spiritual power is available when you're worthy, attracting good without much effort.

Like sunlight, your thoughts can either nurture or block opportunities. Invisible forces are ready to help you, but you must not interfere. These forces work silently, and "you reap what you sow."

You possess immense power within yourself, but many rush through life, missing it. Concentration can revolutionize your life and help you achieve more with ease.

Look within yourself for the greatest power ever made. To speak wisely, focus on the subject at hand. Silence allows deep thoughts to emerge, and wise speech requires practice in silence. The real silence connects you to inner forces and the absolute law.

Practice thought concentration by holding the thought: "In silence, I will allow my higher self to have complete control. I will be true to my higher self. I will live true to my conception of what is right. It is in my self-interest to live up to my best. I demand wisdom to act wisely for myself and others."

In the next chapter, learn about the mysterious law that links humanity together through cooperative thought, choosing companions and friends for you.

Lesson 5

How Concentrated thought Links all Humanity Together

It is within your power to fulfill your every wish. Success is the outcome of your mindset. I will demonstrate how to cultivate a successful mindset.

The ability to govern and attract success resides within yourself. The barriers that obstruct these potentials are under your control. You possess boundless power to think, which serves as the conduit linking you to your all-knowing source.

Success is the consequence of particular mental states or patterns of thinking. These states can be regulated by you and summoned at will.

You have evolved from a humble atom to your current state because of your inherent power to think. This power will always remain with you, propelling you toward perfection. As you progress, you generate new aspirations, which can be realized.

The power to govern lies within you. The impediments that hinder your governance are also within you. These barriers are rooted in ignorance.

Focused thought can achieve seemingly impossible outcomes and actualize your deepest desires. As you dismantle limitations, new ambitions will emerge. You start to experience deliberate thought formations.

It is just as simple to fill your life with what you desire as it is with what you do not desire. The decision lies within your will.

There are no barriers preventing you from obtaining what you desire, as long as your desires align with what is morally right. If you pursue something that is not morally right, you go against the grand plans of the universe and are destined to fail. However, if you base your desires on justice and goodwill, you tap into the supportive energies of universal currents. Instead of facing obstacles, you can rely on eventual success, even if initial circumstances appear bleak.

Do not dwell on temporary appearances; maintain unwavering faith in your ultimate success. Carefully formulate your plans, ensuring they are in harmony with universal justice. The crucial thing to remember is to keep fear, anger, and their associated negative forces at bay.

There is no greater power than the belief stemming from the understanding that your thoughts align with divine laws and the sincere conviction that your cause is just. Although you may achieve temporary results even with unjust causes, these outcomes are fleeting. Eventually, you will need to dismantle your flawed thought structure and rebuild on the foundation of righteousness. Plans founded on falsehoods generate disharmonious vibrations and are inherently self-destructive. Refrain from building until you can build correctly; anything else is a waste of time. You might temporarily set aside your commitment to righteousness, but its true vibrations will disrupt your unjust plans until you are compelled back onto the path of righteousness.

All righteous causes prevail eventually, despite temporary setbacks. Therefore, when you encounter adversity, quell your fears, banish destructive thoughts, and uphold the integrity of your moral and spiritual life.

"Where There Is A Will There Is A Way." This adage holds true because the will can pave a path when given the opportunity to enlist the support of assisting forces. The more the will is cultivated, the higher the path it will lead to.

During times of gloom and discouragement, demonstrate your inner strength by rejoicing in your ability to control your emotions, maintaining calm, serenity, and brightness as if prosperity were already yours.

"Be faithful in sowing the seeds of successful thoughts, trusting that the sun will continue to shine and yield a bountiful harvest in due time."

It's not always necessary to focus on the success of a venture while actively engaged in it. During periods of inactivity, the mind is more liberated to grasp new ideas that can enhance the opportunities being pursued. When you're actively involved in a task, you think within established channels, avoiding the need to redo the work.

In negative moods, intuitions tend to be more active, as thoughts are less controlled by the will. All actions should ideally gain the approval of intuition. Negative moods attract similar thoughts through the law of affinity. Therefore, cultivating thoughts of success is crucial to attract similar positive energies. While this may seem unconventional to those unfamiliar with the concept, there are indeed thought currents that consistently bring about similar ideas.

Understanding the laws of thought, focusing solely on Good, Truth, and Success can lead to more progress with less effort. Forces aiding the mind are often underestimated. Believing in the value of thought and its laws can guide you correctly and enhance your business gains.

To gain better control over your thoughts, when facing fears, reassure your determination that you are not alone, surrounded by invisible forces that will assist in overcoming unfavorable appearances. This affirmation builds courage. The difference between a fearless and fearful person lies in their will and hope. If success is lacking, believe in it, hope for it, and claim it. Apply the same approach to reinforce thoughts of desire, aspiration, imagination, expectation, ambition, understanding, trust, and assurance.

Anxiety, anger, discouragement, indecision, or worry arise when higher powers of the mind aren't cooperating. By exercising your will, you can organize the mind's powers so that your moods change as desired rather than being influenced by external circumstances.

Whether considering what you eat or observing while walking, the key is to concentrate on the current activity. This practice helps control minor actions, preventing the formation of habits that could hinder concentration on more critical tasks later. The ability to concentrate leads to a fulfilling and busy life, where time doesn't drag, and there's always plenty to do. This person avoids dwelling on past mistakes, maintaining a happy demeanor.

Despite our discouragements and failures, if we assert our profound inheritance, "life, truth, and force, like an electric current," will infuse our lives until we embrace our "birthright in eternity."

The will does not operate with clarity, decisiveness, and promptness unless it is cultivated accordingly. Only a few individuals truly understand their actions every minute of the day. This lack of awareness stems from insufficient orderliness and accuracy in observation. However, it is not challenging to maintain awareness of one's actions if concentration is practiced with calm deliberation, fostering clear, prompt, and decisive thinking. Rushing or worrying during tasks prevents clear imprinting on the sensitive canvas of the subconscious mind, leading to a lack of true consciousness of one's actions. Therefore, cultivate accuracy and concentration of thought, along with unwavering honesty, and soon you will master concentration.

Lesson 6

The Training of the Will to Do

The will to do stands as the paramount force in the realm of human accomplishment, and its limits are indeterminable beforehand.

Tasks considered impossible just a few ages ago are now commonplace achievements. Today, the prevailing belief is: "All things are possible."

The Will To Do is a practical force, challenging to define precisely. It can be likened to electricity; we comprehend it solely through its causes and effects. We wield this power, and its direction shapes our destiny. Every time we consciously or unconsciously execute a definite action, we engage the principle of the Will. The Will can be employed for any purpose, whether right or wrong, thus significantly influencing our lives.

Every individual possesses a degree of "Will To Do." This inner energy governs all conscious acts, directing our life forces. Our habits, whether beneficial or detrimental, result from our Will. We elevate or diminish our life circumstances based on our Will. The Will intersects with all realms of knowledge, activity, and achievement.

Consider instances where individuals exhibit extraordinary strength during moments of excitement. For example, a frail farmer's wife single-handedly moved items from a burning house that later required three men to handle. It was her "Will To Do" that enabled her to accomplish this feat.

Genius lies in the Will to meticulously execute small tasks with unwavering diligence. Diligently performed minor tasks pave the way for greater opportunities.

The Will achieves its greatest feats through activities stemming from intense concentration, honing the power of voluntary attention. Mastery of this skill allows us to direct our focus at will and persist steadfastly until our goals are attained. With adept utilization, our Will Power becomes a formidable force capable of achieving nearly anything. It surpasses physical strength because it governs not only the physical but also the mental and moral faculties.

Few possess perfectly developed and balanced Will Power, yet those who do effortlessly overcome their weaknesses. Conduct a thorough self-examination, identifying your greatest weaknesses, and employ your Will Power to conquer them. Gradually eliminate faults until you've forged a resilient character and personality.

Guidelines for Improvement: When a desire arises, assess its merit. If it is detrimental, employ your Will Power to extinguish it. Conversely, if it aligns with righteousness, mobilize your Will Power to surmount obstacles and attain the desired good.

Slowness in Making Decisions. This is a weakness of Will Power. You know you should do something, but you delay doing it due to a lack of decisiveness. It's often easier not to act than to act, but your conscience urges you to take action. The vast majority of people fail because they hesitate to make necessary decisions promptly. Successful individuals seize opportunities by making quick decisions. This power of will can be harnessed to cultivate culture, wealth, and health.

Some Special Pointers. Over the next week, strive to make quicker decisions in your daily affairs. Set a specific time to wake up and adhere to it rigorously. Accomplish tasks promptly or ahead of schedule. While it's important to deliberate on weighty matters, practicing swift decision-making in smaller tasks will enhance your ability to decide quickly on larger issues. Avoid procrastination. Decide promptly, even if there's a risk of making the wrong choice. Practice this approach for a week or two and observe your progress.

The Lack of Initiative. This impediment prevents many from succeeding. They habitually imitate others instead of demonstrating initiative. We often hear phrases like, "He appears intelligent, but lacks initiative." Their lives become monotonous routines, while those who thrive utilize their initiative to enrich their lives. The lack of initiative, the ability to think and act independently, is a significant factor contributing to poverty.

You Are as Good as Anyone. You possess willpower, and if utilized, it can secure your share of life's luxuries. Use it to claim what is rightfully yours. Do not rely on others for assistance; we must fight our own battles. A fighter is admired by all, while a coward is scorned.

Every individual faces unique challenges, so analyze your opportunities, assess your circumstances, and identify your natural abilities. Develop improvement plans and implement them diligently. Do not merely plan; execute your plans decisively. Make specific plans and persist until your objectives are achieved. Implement these suggestions earnestly, and you will witness remarkable results, transforming your entire life. A powerful affirmation for those with noble intentions is: "Through my willpower, I dare to pursue my desires." This affirmation has a profound strengthening effect.

The Spirit of Perseverance. Perseverance is the key to success. Many individuals give up just before reaching their goals. Had they persevered a little longer, they would have triumphed. While some possess initiative, they scatter it across multiple endeavors, diluting its impact. It's crucial to concentrate initiative on a single goal to maximize its effectiveness.

Developing more determination, which is essentially the Will To Do, involves sticking to a task until you achieve results. Before embarking on any endeavor, it's essential to envision the outcome. Choose a path that leads to a tangible destination rather than aimlessly wandering. The journey must yield substantial results of some kind. Many young individuals initiate projects without a clear endpoint in mind. Ultimately, it's not just the beginning but the culmination of a journey that truly matters. Each step should bring you closer to the goal you set out to achieve.

Lack of perseverance is simply the absence of the Will To Do. It requires the same energy to affirm, "I will persist," as it does to concede defeat. The moment you concede, you extinguish your determination. Every time you allow your determination to falter, you diminish its strength. It's crucial to recognize when your determination wanes and concentrate on reinforcing it with sheer Will Power.

Avoid making decisions when your mind is agitated. In moments of anger, impulse overrides reason, leading to regrettable decisions. Success is unattainable if decisions are made while mental faculties are not fully under control. Therefore, adhere to the principle of making decisions only when you are in the best state of mind. If you struggle with a quick temper, regain control by counting backward, which demands concentration and restores calmness, thus breaking the temper habit.

Reflect on your thoughts and actions during moments of anger. Persist until you perceive yourself as others do. Writing out the scene and evaluating the character's behavior can provide valuable insights.

Special Instructions to Develop the Will To Do: Willpower is a form of mental energy that requires the proper mindset to manifest. People often speak of others possessing remarkable willpower, but in reality, it's about utilizing the latent force within oneself. Understand that nobody monopolizes willpower; there is an abundance for all. Willpower is essentially the concentration of mental energy at a single point. Each individual is endowed with the necessary willpower they demand. It's unnecessary to develop willpower if you consistently utilize what you possess. Remember, your life is shaped to a significant extent by the manner in which you employ your will. Failure to do so results in a lack of independence and firmness, rendering you a mere tool for others' use. Learning to harness your will is more important than developing intellect. Individuals who haven't mastered their will often allow others to sway their decisions, leading to indecision and lack of achievement, while those with disciplined willpower rise to become leaders.

Lesson 7

The Concentrated Mental Demand

The Mental Demand is a formidable force in achieving goals. The mindset we adopt influences our facial expressions, dictates actions, alters our physical state, and governs our lives. I won't delve into explaining the silent force that yields results; rather, I aim to assist you in developing your mental faculties to accomplish your objectives. The concentrated Mental Demand harbors remarkable power and potential. Like all forces, it adheres to laws and can be significantly augmented through consecutive, systematic effort.

To harness the power of mental demand, every facet of the mind must be engaged, utilizing every available resource to manifest the desired outcome. Through intense desire, one can eliminate all distractions and focus solely on the objective. By practicing this singular concentration until the goal is achieved, you cultivate a formidable Will capable of realizing any aspiration.

Merely performing ordinary tasks relegates one to the realm of mediocrity. Surpassing others, even by a small margin, elevates you to the ranks of life's achievers. To stand out, you must accomplish more than the average individual. Achieving this is feasible through concentrated focus on your desires and exerting your utmost effort. Success isn't determined by physical prowess or inherent genius; rather, it hinges on the intensity of desire. Analogously, like an engine gradually accelerating to its maximum speed, individuals increase their desire to excel. The one with the greatest intensity of desire emerges victorious, often by a minute margin, yet securing the laurels.

World-renowned successes aren't always individuals with exceptional physical prowess or apparent aptitude. Initially, they may not have appeared well-suited to their circumstances. However, they attained success through unwavering determination, refusing to be disheartened by setbacks or daunted by difficulties. They remained resolute in their pursuit, never losing sight of their goals. Within each of us lies this silent force of extraordinary power. When developed, it can surmount seemingly insurmountable obstacles, propelling us toward greater achievements. The more acquainted we become with this force, the more adept we become as strategists, the greater our courage grows, and the stronger our desire for self-expression across various endeavors.

No one will ever be deemed a failure once they become aware of the silent force within them that shapes their destiny. However, without consciousness of this inner force, clarity of vision is obscured, and external conditions resist the power of the mind. Mental resolve is the key to unlocking achievement. Once formed, it should persistently assert its claim until the desired objective is attained. To ensure the fruition of plans, every faculty of the mind must be employed. Patience, perseverance, and all indomitable forces within must be summoned and utilized with utmost efficacy.

Perseverance stands as the cornerstone of success. To persevere, one must maintain relentless application, concentrating thoughts on the task at hand and channeling every energy toward its accomplishment. Yielding prematurely weakens all future endeavors.

The Mental Demand may seem elusive because of its intangibility, yet it stands as the mightiest force in the world. It is freely available for use, but no one can wield it on your behalf. It is not a mere illusion; it is a potent force that can be employed without cost. In times of doubt, it offers guidance; in moments of uncertainty, it provides clarity; in times of fear, it instills courage. It is the driving force that fuels the energies necessary for achieving one's purpose. Within you lies a vast reservoir of potentialities, and the Mental Demand transforms these possibilities into realities. It furnishes everything needed for accomplishment, selecting the tools and imparting instructions on their use. Every Mental Demand strengthens the brain centers by attracting external forces.

The power of a Mental Demand is often underestimated. It can be so potent that you can convey your thoughts to another without uttering a word. Have you ever experienced discussing a matter with a friend only to find them broaching the subject before you had a chance to speak? Have you ever suggested something to a friend in a letter, only for them to act on it before receiving your correspondence? Have you ever wished to speak to someone, only for them to unexpectedly arrive or call? Such instances of thought responses are common, indicating the profound influence of Mental Demand.

These occurrences are neither coincidences nor accidents but the outcomes of mental demands propelled by strong concentration. Those who never assert their desires obtain little, while resolute demand marks the initial step toward acquiring what one seeks.

The power of Mental Demand appears absolute, with an inexhaustible supply. It projects itself and manifests the necessary conditions and opportunities for achieving one's objectives. However, it is crucial not to overestimate its value or use it for unrighteous purposes. Once a Mental Demand is made, it must remain unwavering; any faltering weakens the connection to one's desires. Therefore, it's imperative to build a firm foundation devoid of doubt. Doubt diminishes the force of demand, and once lost, it's challenging to regain. Hold steadfastly to your demand until your needs are met.

The Power of Mental Demand is not supernatural but a concentrated power accessible to everyone. It requires the development of brain centers, and its outcome is assured when accompanied by strong, resolute determination. Individuals cannot progress significantly until they recognize this force within themselves. Failure to do so limits success in life. It is this intangible essence that sets one individual apart from others and fosters the development of a robust personality.

If you aspire to achieve much, you must demand much. Once the demand is made, anticipate its fulfillment. Our rewards correspond to our efforts, and the Power of Mental Demand has the potential to bring us what we desire. Ultimately, we become what we determine to be, wielding control over our destiny.

Achieving success begins with cultivating the right mental attitude, aligning actions with one's abilities.

Even individuals of average ability, the ordinary people you encounter daily, have the potential for genuine success, independence, and freedom from worry, becoming masters of their own lives. This can be accomplished by focusing on two key principles:

Firstly, maintaining perpetual dissatisfaction with current endeavors and past achievements is crucial. Secondly, nurturing a belief that the word "impossible" does not apply to them is essential. Building confidence in the mind empowers its potential.

Many, especially older individuals, may wonder how to cultivate self-confidence after months or years of discouragement and monotonous routines. How does one break free from the rut of mundane living and embark on endeavors that infuse life with meaning?

The answer lies in the fact that it is indeed possible, as millions have proven. An illustrious example is Littre, honored among the great minds of France for compiling the monumental French dictionary—a testament to his scholarship. Remarkably, Littre began this endeavor when he was over sixty years old.

Lesson 8

Concentration Gives Mental Poise

A well-poised individual is one who can concentrate effectively, while someone whose mind wanders easily is prone to being unsettled. In a state of distraction, wisdom fails to transition from the subconscious to the conscious mind. Achieving mental tranquility is essential for these two aspects of consciousness to harmonize. Concentration brings peace of mind.

To cultivate poise, it's beneficial to engage with literature that has a calming effect. When you sense your composure slipping, simply utter the word "Peace" and hold onto that thought to maintain self-control.

Perfect concentration is unattainable without peace of mind. Therefore, actively pursue thoughts and actions that promote peace until you are at peace with the world. Once this state is achieved, concentration on any task becomes effortless.

A tranquil mind is devoid of timidity, anxiety, fear, or rigidity. Disturbing thoughts hold no sway over you. Instead, envision yourself as a divine spark, a manifestation of the universal principle that permeates all time and space. Recognize your infinite potential as a child of the infinite.

Remind yourself of your capabilities by affirming, "I have the power to do and be whatever I wish." Keeping this thought in mind will provide significant support.

Beware of the mistake of fixating on business matters even when away from work. While concentration is essential for success, becoming enslaved by it and allowing business concerns to intrude into personal time is detrimental. Such preoccupation leads to burnout and premature depletion of life's energies.

Many individuals find themselves unable to fully engage in leisure activities or even rest due to their incessant focus on work. This involuntary concentration is unhealthy and undermines one's well-being. It's crucial to maintain self-control and not let any single thought dominate your mind.

Failure to exercise control over one's concentration ultimately leads to negative consequences, including adverse effects on health. Therefore, it's essential to be able to set aside one task and transition to another when necessary—an exercise in self-mastery.

Concentration Is Paying Attention to a Chosen Thought. Everything that passes before the eye makes an impression on the subconscious mind, but unless you pay attention to some certain thing you will not remember what you saw. For instance, if you walked down a busy street without seeing anything that attracted your particular attention, you could not recall anything you saw. So you see only what attracts your attention. If you work you only see and remember what you think about. When you concentrate on something it absorbs your whole thought.

Self-Study Valuable. Everyone has some habits that can be overcome by concentration. We will say, for instance, you are in the habit of complaining, or finding fault with yourself or others; or imagining that you do not possess the ability of others; or feeling that you are not as good as someone else; or that you cannot rely on yourself; or harboring any similar thoughts or thoughts of weakness. These should be cast aside and instead thoughts of strength should be put in their place. Just remember every time you think of yourself as being weak, in some way you are making yourself so by thinking you are. Our mental conditions make us what we are. Just watch yourself and see how much time you waste in worrying, fretting, and complaining. The more of it you do, the worse off you are.

Just the minute you are aware of thinking a negative thought, immediately change to a positive one. If you start to think of failure, change to thinking of success. You have the germ of success within you. Care for it the same as the setting hen broods over the eggs and you can make it a reality.

You can make those that you come in contact with feel as you do because you radiate vibrations of the way you feel and your vibrations are felt by others. When you concentrate on a certain thing you turn all the rays of your vibrations on this. Thought is the directing power of all Life's vibrations. If a person should enter a room with a lot of people and feel as if he were a person of no consequence, no one would know he was there unless they saw him, and even if they did, they would not remember seeing him because they were not attracted towards him. But let him enter the room feeling that he was magnetic and concentrating on this thought, others would feel his vibration. So remember the way you feel you can make others feel. This is the law. Make yourself a concentrated dynamo from which your thoughts vibrate to others. Then you are a power in the world. Cultivate the art of feeling, for as I said before you can only make others feel what you feel.

If you will study all of the great characters of history you will find that they were enthusiastic. First, they were enthusiastic themselves, and then they could arouse others' enthusiasm. It is latent in everyone. It is a wonderful force when once aroused. All public men to be a success have to possess it. Cultivate it by concentration. Set aside some hour of the day, wherein to hold rapt converse with the soul. Meditate with sincere desire and contrite heart and you will be able to accomplish that which you have meditated on. This is the keynote of success.

"Think, speak and act just as you wish to be, And you will be that which you wish to be."

You are just what you think you are and not what you may appear to be. You may fool others but not yourself. You may control your life and actions just as you can control your hands. If you want to raise your hand you must first think of raising it. If you want to control your life you must first control your thinking. Easy to do, is it not? Yes, it is, if you will but concentrate on what you think about.

For he only can
That says he will.

How can we secure concentration? To this question, the first and last answer must be: By interest and strong motive. The stronger the motive the greater the concentration.--Eustace Miller, M. D.

The Successful Lives Are the Concentrated Lives. The utterly helpless multitude that sooner or later have to be cared for by charity are those that were never able to concentrate, and who have become the victims of negative ideas.

Train yourself so you will be able to centralize your thought and develop your brain power, and increase your mental energy, or you can be a slacker, a drifter, a quitter or a sleeper. It all depends on how you concentrate, or centralize your thoughts. Your thinking then becomes a fixed power and you do not waste time thinking about something that would not be good for you. You pick out the thoughts that will be the means of bringing you what you desire, and they become a material reality. Whatever we create in the thought world will some day materialize. That is the law. Don't forget this.

In the old days men drifted without concentration but this is a day of efficiency and therefore all of our efforts must be concentrated, if we are to win any success worth the name.

Why People Often Do Not Get What They Concentrate On. Because they sit down in hopeless despair and expect it to come to them.

But if they will just reach out for it with their biggest effort they will find it is within their reach. No one limits us but ourselves. We are what we are today as the result of internal conditions. We can control the external conditions. They are subject to our will.

Through our concentration we can attract what we want, because we become en rapport with the Universal forces, from which we can get what we want.

You have watched races no doubt. They all line up together. Each has his mind set on getting to the goal before the others. This is one kind of concentration. A man starts to think on a certain subject. He has all kinds of thoughts come to him, but by concentration he shuts out all these but the one he has chosen. Concentration is just a case of willing to do a certain thing and doing it.

If you want to accomplish anything first put yourself in a concentrating, reposeful, receptive, acquiring frame of mind. In tackling unfamiliar work make haste slowly and deliberately and then you will secure that interior activity, which is never possible when you are in a hurry or under a strain. When you "think hard" or try to hurry results too quickly, you generally shut off the interior flow of thoughts and ideas. You have often no doubt tried hard to think of something but could not, but just as soon as you stopped trying to think of it, it came to you.

Lesson 9

Concentration can Overcome Bad Habits

Habits play a significant role in shaping our lives, more so than we often acknowledge. They can either be a powerful ally or a formidable enemy of concentration. It's crucial to learn how to overcome habits that hinder concentration and cultivate those that enhance it.

The majority of people are governed by their habits, often unaware of how these habits influence their actions. They perform tasks in certain ways simply out of habit, without considering if there might be a better approach. The goal of this chapter is to encourage you to focus on your habits, distinguishing between those that are beneficial and those that are detrimental. By making necessary adjustments, even harmful habits can be turned into beneficial ones, while good habits can be further improved.

It's important to realize that all habits are shaped consciously or unconsciously by the will. Habit formation occurs gradually through repetition. The more a behavior is repeated, the stronger the habit becomes and the more deeply ingrained it becomes in one's nature. Breaking a long-standing habit can be challenging, but it's possible through strong concentration on adopting its opposite.

"Our life, in its current form, is largely composed of habits—practical, emotional, and intellectual—systematically organized, leading us inevitably toward our destiny, whatever it may be."

We are creatures of habit, constantly imitating and replicating our past behaviors. Each repetition of a behavior leaves a mark, making it easier to repeat in the future. Our intellect and will, though spiritual functions, are influenced by our physical brains, allowing habits of thought and will to form based on our actions. Our nervous systems are shaped by our past behaviors, contributing to the formation of habits.

As we age, our habits solidify, and we become increasingly like automatic machines, following familiar patterns of behavior. Others come to expect us to behave in certain ways, illustrating the significant impact our habits have on our lives. Given that forming good habits is as easy as forming bad ones, we should strive to cultivate only positive habits. Ultimately, we are responsible for our habits, and realizing the importance of forming the right habits can lead to a happier and more successful life.

While habits are typically formed more quickly in youth, it's never too late to start cultivating positive habits. The time to begin controlling our habits is now, as we will never be any younger.

Remember the following maxims:

First Maxim: "We must make our nervous system our ally instead of our enemy."

Second Maxim: "In the acquisition of a new habit as in the leaving off of an old one, we must take care to launch ourselves with as strong and decided an initiative as possible."

The man who consistently does the right thing from boyhood develops only good motives. Therefore, it is crucial for you to concentrate diligently on habits that reinforce positive motives. Surround yourself with every possible aid and avoid forming bad habits, as they can lead to undesirable outcomes. Make a fresh start today by studying why you have been engaging in certain behaviors. If they are not beneficial, avoid them from now on. Resist every temptation, as giving in strengthens the chain of bad habits. Keeping a resolution breaks this chain and strengthens your resolve.

Third Maxim: "Never allow an exception to occur until the new habit is securely rooted in your life."

This maxim emphasizes the importance of remaining steadfast until the new habit is firmly established. There are conflicting inclinations—one to stand firm and the other to give in. Strengthen your willpower through repetition to overcome any opposition.

Fourth Maxim: "Seize the very first possible opportunity to act on every resolution you make, and on every emotional prompting you may experience in the direction of the habits you aspire to gain."

Keeping resolutions is essential, as they not only benefit you directly but also help form the habit of following through on commitments. The brain adapts to these actions, reinforcing the habit. Keeping resolutions, regardless of their significance, is crucial for building this habit.

Fifth Maxim: "Keep the faculty of effort alive in you by a little gratuitous exercise every day."

Regular exercise of the will enhances your ability to control your habits. Engage in challenging tasks occasionally to prepare yourself for difficult situations. This practice acts as insurance against future challenges, ensuring that you remain steadfast and resilient amidst adversity.

The young should be encouraged to focus on their habits and understand that neglecting them can lead to harmful consequences. Youth is a malleable stage of life and should be utilized to establish a solid foundation for a bright future.

The significance of habits, whether for good or bad, cannot be overstated. "Habit is the deepest law of human nature." No individual is immune to the influence of their habits, as they either contribute to their strength or diminish it.

Our tendency towards habits is rooted in their efficiency; once formed, they demand less mental and physical effort. The more ingrained a habit becomes, the more automatic it is. Hence, habit serves as a natural economizer, reducing the need for constant vigilance. For instance, when crossing a busy street, our habit of stopping and looking prevents accidents. Similarly, a chauffeur's ability to operate a vehicle safely relies on ingrained habits. In emergencies, these habits enable quick, automatic responses, reducing risk, fatigue, and errors.

However, it's crucial not to become enslaved by trivial habits. Overcoming undesirable habits requires two key elements: training the willpower to do what is necessary and making a firm resolution to replace the bad habit with a good one. With a strong will, one can diligently focus on eliminating the bad habit, allowing the good habit to take its place quickly.

To overcome a habit, one must approach it with determination and resolve, treating it like a formidable adversary. Bad habits are insidious and relentless, requiring a fierce determination to eradicate them.

In challenging times, when life seems against us, we may inadvertently acquire harmful habits. Yet, even in these moments, making a concerted effort to think and act positively can yield profound results. Despite feeling overwhelmed, the smallest effort is bolstered by a tremendous inner power, lifting us to new realizations.

Our greatest progress often occurs amidst trials and misfortunes, when we recognize our connection to a greater power. By living in accordance with this power, nothing in life can permanently harm us. We possess unlimited internal power, ready to manifest itself when needed. Instead of acting impulsively, it is wiser to wait for guidance from within, allowing us to act with clarity and purpose.

Lesson 10

Achieving Business Success through Concentration

Success in business is seldom a matter of chance, just as failure isn't merely a stroke of luck. Many failures could have been foreseen if the founders had been studied beforehand. Starting a profitable business often requires adjustments and changes along the way. Plans rarely unfold exactly as anticipated; they may need to be adapted and expanded as your business grows. As you broaden your business scope, you also expand your ability to achieve success. This process fosters a deep and unwavering desire to make your business thrive.

When initiating a business venture, your initial concept may be vague. You must refine and fill in the details as you progress, focusing your concentration on each aspect. As you address one issue after another, new opportunities will emerge, leading to further endeavors.

Every fulfilled desire gives rise to another, but failing to act on the first desire stifles subsequent ones. Merely dreaming without taking action leads nowhere. Pure, intense, and sustained desire serves as a potent creative force, propelling us to action and strengthening our resolve when materialized.

Success is earned through diligent effort. Initially, we may lack the knowledge to tackle the challenges ahead, but by doing our best at each task, we develop the capability to handle greater responsibilities. Mastery in business comes from excelling in every endeavor we undertake. A thorough understanding of one's business enables effective direction and oversight. A skilled business leader can monitor operations from afar and intervene when necessary to ensure tasks are completed promptly and accurately.

Business success hinges on focused and concerted efforts. Utilize all mental faculties at your disposal, as their usage enhances their capabilities. The more you accomplish today, the greater your resources for solving tomorrow's challenges.

If you currently work for someone else but aspire to start your own business, carefully consider your desired path. Once you've determined your goal, commit to it wholeheartedly. Behind every desire, there must be effort to bring it to fruition. Maintain unwavering determination to realize your ambitions, channeling your thoughts and actions towards their attainment.

Visualize yourself as successful, believe in your capabilities, and adopt an attitude that commands recognition. Embrace ambitious endeavors with determination and pursue methods you believe will yield results. Even if initial success eludes you, aim high, knowing that any progress is significant.

What others have achieved, you can achieve too. You might even accomplish what others haven't been able to. Always keep a strong desire to succeed in your mind. Be passionate about your goals and endeavors, and ensure they align with benefiting as many people as possible. With this mindset, your life can never be deemed a failure.

To make the most out of life, cultivate a successful business attitude. Expect greatness from both yourself and others. This attitude alone often leads individuals to excel, reaching their fullest potential.

Consistent effort, not sporadic bursts, is what matters on the journey to success. Spurts of energy tire you out and make it difficult to keep going.

Trust your own judgment; it's as valid as anyone else's. Once you reach a decision, stick to it firmly. Doubts and hesitations diminish the value of your judgment. Learning from mistakes and making decisions based on what you believe is right leads to a balanced mind and better outcomes. Others will trust and rely on someone who is decisive and consistent, rather than someone who constantly changes their mind.

In the business world, uncertainties are viewed unfavorably. Reliable firms prefer to work with individuals known for their firmness, judgment, and reliability. Your greatest asset when starting a business, aside from good health, is a solid reputation.

Building a successful business isn't difficult if you can focus all your mental energy on it. It's those who are indecisive and unsure about their goals who struggle. People often say that business is taxing on the nerves, but it's the stress and uncertainty that wear you down, not the business itself. Executing plans may be tiring, but enjoyment comes with rest. As long as you don't overexert yourself, your body's restorative powers will replenish your energy.

By attending to each day's work properly, you develop the capacity to do greater work tomorrow. It's this gradual development that makes big plans achievable. The person who figures out something to do each hour of the day makes progress. Each day should bring you closer to your goal. Keep the idea in mind that you're moving forward; every day must mark progress, and you must keep moving forward once you've started, even if you're not sure of the exact direction.

Even brilliant individuals often underestimate their potential. You shouldn't think an aim is impossible just because it hasn't been achieved before. Every day, someone accomplishes something new. Our progress is accelerating. In the past, it took decades to build a large business, but now it can happen in just a few years, sometimes even months.

Carefully plan each day's activities, and you can reach any height you aim for. When you approach each task with focused thought, you'll produce excellent quality work in large quantities. Decide how much work you'll do each day, and you'll be surprised at how much more you accomplish compared to days when you had no specific goals. I've shown that the average business can achieve the same amount of work in six hours as they currently do in eight, without using more energy. Never start something in an indecisive, uncertain way. Approach everything with confidence and seriousness, focusing your mind and attracting the best associated thoughts. Soon, you'll find you have extra time to plan even bigger things.

A natural leader attracts ideas on their chosen subject through the law of mental attraction, drawing upon the thoughts of others. This is incredibly helpful. Proper training allows you to benefit from others' thoughts, and if you generate valuable ideas yourself, others will benefit from yours. We inherit knowledge from past generations, but we must know how to use it effectively.

A confident, determined person influences everyone around them, inspiring similar qualities in others. You feel compelled to follow their example, as they ignite the same drive within you that propels them forward.

Rarely does someone succeed when they approach tasks with a lackluster attitude. To build a business, you must envision its expansion in your mind before it becomes tangible. Every great achievement started as a mere vision in the creator's mind, with details meticulously worked out from the initial concept. Once a clear idea formed, tangible accomplishments followed.

Modern businesspeople don't just build for the present; they plan ahead. Failure to do so leads to falling behind competitors who are forward-thinking. Today's progressive businesses are the result of careful past planning. That's why young entrepreneurs often achieve more in a few years than their predecessors did in a lifetime.

Feeling drained by your work indicates a mismatch between your efforts and your true calling. Engage in work you love and support causes you believe in. This way, you'll produce your best work and find joy in your endeavors. By growing and developing yourself, you also provide genuine service to humanity.

Success in business isn't random; it's the outcome of scientific ideas and progressive management. Utilize your mental faculties to grow and develop. Remember, everything you do stems from mental activity, giving you full control over your actions. Don't shy away from challenges; your success depends on how you use your mind, which is capable of remarkable development. Encourage those around you to broaden their horizons, and you'll expand your own perspective on life.

Do you fear responsibilities? To develop as an individual, you must embrace responsibilities and demonstrate the law of supply. The world is your rightful sphere of activity. How much of a conqueror are you? Are you avoiding responsibilities? Your higher self never flinches, so embrace responsibility and allow your higher self to manifest. You'll find strength and satisfaction in tackling challenging tasks head-on.

Lesson II

Concentrate on Courage

Courage is the foundation of a person's character. A courageous individual possesses persistence; they voice their beliefs and act upon them. Courage instills confidence and attracts other moral and mental strengths, shaping a resilient individual. Conversely, lacking courage draws weaknesses like indecision, doubt, and wavering purpose. Concentrating on courage is thus crucial for success.

The absence of courage leads to financial, mental, and moral challenges. Instead of viewing new problems as opportunities, the courage-lacking tend to see barriers, leading to inevitable failure. This concept warrants thorough exploration. By regarding everything within one's power as achievable, rather than merely probable, one accomplishes more. Considering something impossible attracts failure, undermining confidence and determination.

The courageless inadvertently attract contemptible, weakening, and destructive elements, blaming fate when they fail to attain their desires. Courage involves having strong desires, backed by mental strength, capable of overcoming unfavorable conditions. A courageous individual commands situations, whether in battle or business.

Courage is essentially the will to act. It requires no more energy than cowardice but demands proper training. Courage focuses mental forces on tasks, directing them purposefully and steadily towards success. Cowardice disperses mental and moral strength, inviting failure.

As creatures of habit, we should avoid those lacking courage, evident in their fear of confronting new challenges. A courageous person is never afraid.

Start today with the conviction that there's no reason not to be courageous. Discard fear-inducing thoughts promptly. Cultivate the habit of positive thinking and affirm your courage when faced with difficulties. Remember, as the master of your mind, you control your thoughts. Embrace courage because you desire it, need it, use it, and reject cowardice.

There's no excuse for losing courage. The challenges overcome with courage far outweigh those succumbed to without it. Therefore, the moralist is right in saying that the only thing to fear is fear itself.

Never allow someone else's opinion to sway you; they can't comprehend your abilities or the potential of your forces. You won't truly know yourself until you put yourself to the test, so how could anyone else know? Don't let others determine your worth.

Many remarkable achievements were deemed impossible until they were proven otherwise. Understanding this principle makes all things possible. If they were truly impossible, we wouldn't even conceive of them.

The moment you let someone influence you against your beliefs, you lose the confidence and courage that drive success. Yielding to another's plan diminishes your own resolve and makes you reliant on their direction. This lack of self-reliance invites failure. When you allow others to sway you from your path, you lose your own courage and determination without gaining any in return, akin to surrendering all your possessions without receiving anything in exchange.

Focus on the opposite of fear, want, poverty, and sickness. Never doubt your abilities; you have plenty if you use them. Many fail because they doubt their capacity, letting fear thoughts weaken them. Fear stifles energy and prevents success. Few people realize their full potential, but those who believe in themselves develop the courage to overcome obstacles and achieve their goals.

Courage is available to you; believe in it, claim it, and use it. Believe in the success of your business, assert it, and work diligently to make it so. Difficulties fade in the face of courage. A courageous individual can inspire others because courage, like cowardice, is contagious.

Courageous individuals overcome life's trials, command success, make sound judgments, and develop influential characters. They often become leaders in the communities they serve.

To overcome depression and melancholia, focus on your higher self, disconnecting from harmful forces. You can shift your mood by concentrating on positive subjects. With willpower and thought control, you can achieve anything. We all possess inherent power, and fear is typically rooted in ignorance.

Evil stems from ignorance, but we have the power to overcome it through thought. Pain from wrongdoing serves as a lesson to recognize our ignorance. Depression arises when our thoughts attract negative forces.

To counter this, exercise your willpower and concentrate on uplifting topics. Focus solely on subjects worthy of your higher self and its abilities. By doing so, you can shift your mindset and overcome depression and melancholia.

Lesson 12

Concentrate on Wealth

It was never intended for man to be poor. When wealth is obtained under proper conditions, it enriches life. Everything holds value and can be used for good or ill. Like wealth, the forces of the mind can be directed positively or negatively. A little rest rejuvenates, but excessive rest leads to laziness and idle daydreams.

Wealth acquired unjustly is a misuse of one's abilities, but wealth obtained through rightful means brings blessings. Through wealth, we can uplift ourselves and humanity.

For many, wealth is a goal that drives their efforts. They seek it to improve their appearance and surroundings, which in turn attract friends. Surrounding ourselves with attractive environments and influences fosters inspiration and proper thought.

To begin acquiring wealth, surround yourself with supportive influences and immerse yourself in a cultured environment. Most great individuals throughout history have been relatively affluent; money, whether earned or inherited, enables them to accomplish their goals.

Wealth often results from achievement, not just hard work. Thousands toil tirelessly but never amass wealth, while others achieve it with less effort. Recognizing opportunities is crucial for wealth acquisition. Without utilizing mental faculties, one remains a laborer, directed by those who harness their mental powers effectively.

Saving from earnings alone rarely leads to wealth within a lifetime. Many spend their lives scrimping and saving, depleting vitality and energy in the process. For instance, a man who walks to work to save money may waste valuable time. While he saves a small amount daily, the time spent walking could be more profitably invested in improving his business prospects.

The same effort directed towards overcoming business challenges could lead him towards prosperity.

One of the significant mistakes made by many individuals in the current generation is that they associate with those who fail to bring out or develop the best within them. When the social aspect of life is overly emphasized, and recreation or entertainment becomes the primary focus, individuals develop habits of extravagance rather than economy. These habits lead to the wasteful use of physical, mental, moral, and spiritual resources instead of their conservation. Consequently, they lack proper motivation, and their God-given powers and forces remain undeveloped. This lack of development inevitably results in poor judgment in higher life relationships. Financially, they often find themselves lean, at times functioning as parasites, and always, given the opportunity, consuming more than they produce.

It seems tragic that individuals must endure such painful lessons before understanding the forces and laws that govern life. Few learn from the mistakes of others; they must experience these hardships firsthand and then apply the gained knowledge to reconstruct their lives.

Any man who has ever amounted to anything has never solely engaged in detailed work for extended periods. He requires time for reflection and improvement. His approach to duties evolves through deliberate and concentrated effort, as he constantly strives to enhance his methods.

The other day, I attended a lecture on Prosperity delivered by a lecturer who had been practically broke for ten years. Curious about his teachings, I asked him if he believed in his maxims and if they had made him prosperous. Despite his belief in his teachings, he admitted they hadn't made him prosperous. When I examined his circumstances, I uncovered how poverty had been his constant companion. His actions and beliefs attracted poverty, as he dressed poorly and held lectures in unimpressive settings. I explained to him the power of thoughts, emphasizing that thoughts of wealth attract wealth, while thoughts of poverty attract poverty. By instilling thoughts of wealth into his mental forces and utilizing external conditions to support them, he could change his circumstances.

Many people believe that having money makes it easy to accumulate more. However, this isn't always the case. Ninety percent of men who start in business fail, indicating that money alone doesn't guarantee success. It requires training to seek and utilize good investment opportunities. Those who inherit money often lose it, while those who earn it not only understand its value but also develop the ability to use it effectively and generate more if lost.

Business success today relies on foresight, good judgment, grit, firm resolution, and settled purpose. However, never underestimate the power of thought, which is as real a force as electricity. Ensure that your thoughts are positive and beneficial, as what you send out should be as good as what you receive. Failing to enrich others with your thoughts will hinder your own enrichment.

Individuals who selfishly try to gain from others without giving back become mean and ultimately fail to enjoy their acquisitions. It's a cycle where what we take from others will eventually be taken from us. All obligations must be met fairly for us to reach perfection in our lives. Thus, it's essential to willingly provide fair exchanges for all that we receive.

Surrounding oneself with positive influences, including good thoughts, health, home and business environments, and successful associates, is crucial in acquiring wealth. Cultivate relationships with individuals of substantial caliber and align your thought vibrations regarding business with theirs. This will not only make your company agreeable but also sought after. Establishing intimate friendships with reputable, wealthy individuals allows for investment of surplus earnings until you've developed the initiative and business acumen to manage your own investments successfully. Through such associations, you'll find your place in life among individuals of significance.

With financial security achieved, derive satisfaction from using part of it to facilitate the journey for those who follow. In every brain lies the potential energy to propel oneself out of stagnation and onto the path of success if harnessed correctly. Just as gasoline in a car's engine remains inert until sparked, the energy in the human mind awaits activation. Hope, self-confidence, and determination serve as the sparks that ignite this energy, enabling individuals to overcome obstacles and achieve success, regardless of their level of genius.

Lesson 13

You can Concentrate, but Will You?

Everyone possesses the ability to concentrate, but whether you choose to utilize it is entirely up to you. Merely having the capability is not enough; you must take action. There exists far more untapped potential than actualized ability. Why do many people with potential fail to achieve success? While circumstances may vary, the responsibility typically lies with the individual. Despite having opportunities, many fail to capitalize on them.

Reflect on what you desire to achieve but haven't yet pursued. If you feel you should be progressing further, examine why you haven't. Sometimes, even minor obstacles hinder success. Identify the root cause of your shortcomings and failures. Have you been waiting for someone to guide you or pave the way? If so, shift your focus to a new mindset.

Success requires two essential elements: energy and a strong will to succeed. Nothing can replace these. Expecting an easy path is unrealistic; challenges and setbacks build resilience and moral strength. Those who live passively lack these qualities, having never confronted adversity. We must actively create favorable conditions rather than passively waiting for them to materialize.

The path to success involves overcoming obstacles and disproving naysayers. Perseverance is unstoppable. While challenges may obscure the path, they can all be overcome with determination and focused effort. Conversely, believing obstacles to be insurmountable leads to half-hearted attempts and eventual failure.

Many individuals hesitate to begin unless success is assured—a grave error. Certainty of success is rare; circumstances change, and obstacles arise unexpectedly. The key is to maintain courage and seek alternative routes when faced with roadblocks. Approach tasks with unwavering determination to utilize your full potential, as this concentrated effort yields success.

Most people are beaten before they start. They anticipate obstacles and focus on them rather than on finding ways to overcome them. Consequently, they unwittingly magnify their obstacles instead of diminishing them. Have you ever undertaken something that you thought would be hard, only to find it surprisingly easy afterward? This is often the case. Challenges that seem daunting at first are often conquered with ease once confronted. Therefore, embark on your journey with the belief that the path will be clear, and if it's not, you'll clear the way. Every successful individual has cleared their path, often without the assistance available today.

The key to success is to steadfastly pursue your goals. Don't waver from your path, but resolve to accomplish what you set out to do. Don't be discouraged by setbacks, as they cannot deter a determined individual—the one who understands that success requires tremendous resolution, concentrated effort, and whole-hearted dedication.

As Goethe said, "He who has a firm will, molds the world to himself." Similarly, Victor Hugo noted, "People do not lack strength; they lack Will." Success is not solely determined by skill but by activity and unwavering determination. For the individual who gives their best effort, failure is not an option.

No matter what you are currently working on, don't lose courage. The tides of fortune are ever-changing, and if you are willing and ambitious, they will turn in your favor eventually.

Work is essential for personal development and increasing courage. Without it, life would become monotonous.

To those who seek advancement, I say: don't see your present position as permanent. Continuously develop the qualities that will aid you when opportunities arise. Be vigilant and alert for opportunities, for we attract what we focus on. If you are the right person for the job, someone is seeking you out. When they find you, give your full attention, demonstrate your ability to concentrate, and show no signs of fear, uncertainty, or doubt. A confident individual is destined for success, regardless of circumstances.

☸☸☸

Lesson 14

The Art of Concentrating by Means of Practical Exercises

Select a thought and see how long you can focus your mind on it. It's helpful to have a clock initially to track the time. For example, if you choose to contemplate health, you can derive significant benefits from this practice besides enhancing concentration. Regard health as the greatest blessing in the world. Don't allow any other thoughts to intrude. The moment another thought tries to surface, dismiss it immediately.

Make it a daily habit to concentrate on this thought for about ten minutes. Keep practicing until you can maintain focus to the exclusion of everything else. Centralizing your thoughts on health will prove immensely valuable. Regardless of your current condition, visualize yourself as you desire to be, and disregard any contrary thoughts. Initially, it might be challenging to overcome negative thoughts, especially if you have ailments. However, with practice, you'll be able to shut out these negative thoughts and envision yourself in a state of wellness. Each time you concentrate, you refine the image of health within you, and as you internalize this image, you become healthier, stronger, and more vibrant.

It's crucial to understand the significance of forming mental images. Successful individuals throughout history have utilized this technique, albeit few recognize its full importance. Your actions are continuously influenced by the mental images you create. If you allow negative images to dominate your thoughts, you inadvertently cultivate a negative disposition. Your external reality will mirror your internal thoughts. Whatever you consistently focus on in your mind will manifest in your external world.

Deep concentration connects you with the creative spirit of the universe, allowing creative energy to flow through you and manifest your creations into reality. In this state, your mind synchronizes with the infinite, registering cosmic intelligence and receiving its messages. You become infused with cosmic energy, experiencing a flood of divine power. This heightened state of consciousness aligns you with the supra-consciousness, which registers higher cosmic vibrations and is often likened to a wireless station receiving messages from the universal mind.

Few individuals reach this level of concentration, and many are unaware of its possibility. They mistakenly believe that concentration implies limiting oneself to a single subject. However, the deeper concentration that aligns us with the Infinite is what fosters and sustains health.

Once you have experienced contact with your supra-consciousness, you become the master of your human thoughts. The insights that come to you surpass mere human thoughts and are often referred to as Cosmic Consciousness. Once this state is attained, it is indelibly etched into your consciousness. Achieving this state requires significant training, but with practice, it becomes increasingly attainable, and over time, you can harness powers previously unknown to you. In this heightened state of concentration, you possess the ability to direct the expression of almost infinite power.

Consider the analogy of the sun's rays focused through a magnifying glass. When concentrated on an object, the heat produced far exceeds that of the scattered rays. Similarly, when you focus your attention on a single object, every action, voluntary and involuntary, aligns with the pursuit of that object. By directing your energies exclusively towards a goal, you generate the force necessary to manifest your desires.

Focusing your thoughts amplifies their strength. Although the exercises that follow may seem tedious and monotonous, they are incredibly beneficial. With persistence, you will discover their immense value in enhancing your powers of concentration.

Before delving into the exercises, let's address a common concern: fatigue after a day of work. Despite feeling exhausted, engaging in mental exercises is still possible. After returning home and having dinner, individuals often find their work-related thoughts persisting, hindering their ability to rest. It's widely accepted that specific thoughts activate particular sets of brain cells, leaving others idle and in need of rest. By engaging in activities or thoughts divergent from those of the workday, you allow tired cells to recuperate while stimulating previously unused ones. By redirecting your attention to new thoughts, you alleviate the strain on tired cells and facilitate their much-needed rest. Meanwhile, the dormant cells, eager for activity, find fulfillment, allowing you to enjoy your evenings while ensuring adequate rest.

Once you've mastered controlling your thoughts, changing them becomes as effortless as changing clothes. The key to concentration lies in the ability to exclude external thoughts and focus solely on the intended subject. To achieve this, begin by gaining control over your body, then your mind, and ultimately your will. Recognize the strength of your will and understand that it is capable of achieving anything. Strengthen your mind by aligning it with the will, enhancing its capacity as a transmitter of thoughts through increased force.

The optimal time for deep concentration is after immersing yourself in something inspiring, as it elevates you mentally and spiritually to the desired state. At this juncture, you are primed for profound concentration. Begin by ensuring your surroundings are conducive to relaxation. Open the windows for fresh air, then lie flat on your bed without a pillow, ensuring every muscle is completely relaxed. Breathe slowly and deeply, filling your lungs with fresh air, and hold the breath comfortably before exhaling slowly in a rhythmic manner. Continue this breathing exercise for five minutes, allowing the Divine Breath to flow through you, cleansing and rejuvenating every cell of your brain and body.

Once you've completed this preparatory phase, contemplate how serene and relaxed you feel. Let yourself become enthralled by the idea of receiving knowledge surpassing anything you've experienced before. Relax and allow the spirit to work within and through you, guiding you toward accomplishing your desired goals.

Banish any doubts or fears from your mind and instead, believe wholeheartedly that your desires will manifest. In the realm of thought, the moment you wish for something, it is already realized. Maintain the conviction that your concentration efforts will yield success, and do not allow any distractions to interfere. With perseverance, you will soon master the art of concentration, unlocking your ability to achieve anything you set your mind to.

Before delving into concentration exercises, it's essential to train your body to obey the commands of the mind. Begin by gaining control over your muscular movements. The following exercise is particularly effective in helping you attain perfect control over your muscles.

Exercise 1

Sit comfortably in a chair and attempt to remain perfectly still. Though seemingly simple, this task requires focused attention to avoid involuntary muscular movements. With practice, you'll discover the ability to sit motionless for fifteen minutes. Initially, start with five minutes in a relaxed position, gradually increasing to ten, then fifteen minutes. Avoid straining yourself; complete relaxation is essential. Cultivating the habit of relaxation is highly beneficial.

Exercise 2

Sit with your head up, chin out, and shoulders back in a chair. Raise your right arm to shoulder level, pointing to your right, and fix your gaze on your fingers while keeping the arm still for one minute. Repeat the exercise with your left arm. Gradually increase the duration to five minutes for each arm. Ensure your hand is palm-down, the easiest position. By keeping your eyes fixed on your fingertips, you can gauge the steadiness of your arm.

Exercise 3

Hold a small glass of water by the fingers and extend the arm directly in front of you. Fix your eyes on the glass and endeavor to keep the arm perfectly steady without any noticeable movement. Begin with one minute and gradually extend to five. Perform the exercise with each arm.

Exercise 4

Observe yourself throughout the day to prevent muscle tension or strain. Aim to maintain an easy and relaxed demeanor, cultivating self-possession instead of appearing nervous or strained. This mental composure will enhance your posture and demeanor. Eliminate unnecessary gestures and body movements, indicative of inadequate body control. After mastering this control, notice the lack of poise in individuals who haven't attained it. Reflecting on a recent interaction with a salesman, I observed continual body movements and thought about suggesting that he communicate verbally rather than relying on excessive body language. Observing others during interactions can reveal their lack of poise.

To eliminate any habits of twitching or jerking your body, focus on the thought "I will not" whenever you notice these involuntary movements. Practice self-control when encountering disruptive noises, considering them as exercises in self-discipline rather than allowing them to upset you. Such exercises can be found throughout your daily routine.

The purpose of the preceding exercises is to gain mastery over involuntary muscular movements, making your actions entirely voluntary. The following exercises are designed to bring your voluntary muscles under the control of your will, allowing your mental forces to govern your physical movements.

Exercise 5

Position your chair near a table, place your hands on it, and clench your fists with the back of the hand on the table and the thumb folded over the fingers. Focus your gaze on the fist and gradually extend the thumb, concentrating on the movement as if it were crucial. Continue extending each finger one by one until they are all open, then reverse the process, closing the fingers in reverse order until the fist returns to its original position with the thumb closed over the fingers. Repeat this exercise with each hand, starting with one hand and then the other, gradually increasing repetitions from five to ten times with each hand.

Initially, these exercises may cause fatigue, but it's crucial to practice them regularly to train your attention and gain control over muscular movements. Keep your focus on each movement of the hand to derive maximum benefit from the exercise.

Exercise 6

Place your right hand on your knee, with all fingers and the thumb closed except for the first finger, which points out in front of you. Slowly move the finger from side to side while keeping your attention fixed on its end. You can create variations of such exercises, ensuring they are simple and that your attention remains firmly fixed on the moving body part. Your attention may attempt to wander to something more engaging, but these exercises are valuable for practicing attention control and ensuring it stays focused where needed.

You might initially perceive these exercises as simple and of little value, but I assure you that in a short time, you will notice a significant improvement in your control over muscular movements, posture, demeanor, and attention span. You'll find that you can concentrate more effectively on tasks at hand, which is incredibly valuable.

Regardless of what you're doing, imagine that it is your primary focus in life, as if nothing else in the world matters but the task at hand. Resist the urge to let your attention wander away from your work, even though it may rebel initially. Conquering your rebellious attention is a significant victory that you'll appreciate many times over in the future. Practice concentrating on mundane and uninteresting objects daily, as this strengthens your ability to focus. Choose objects that are not inherently captivating, as they require more attention and provide better exercise for concentration.

Mastering concentration enables you to gain full control over your body and mind, becoming the master of your inclinations rather than their slave. With self-control, you can influence and control others, developing a formidable willpower that sets you apart from those who lack it. Strive for excellence in all your endeavors, never settling for mediocrity. When you achieve this level of control, you become the person you were meant to be.

Exercise 7

Concentration Enhances the Sense of Smell. During walks, drives in the countryside, or encounters with flower gardens, focus your attention on the scents of flowers and plants. Try to identify as many different odors as possible, then select one specific scent and concentrate solely on it. This focused attention significantly heightens your sense of smell but requires a particularly attentive mindset. Shut out all thoughts except those related to the odor you're concentrating on, and ignore all other scents. Practice these exercises regularly to develop your sense of smell, recalling the circumstances of each exercise when you encounter similar scents in the future.

The purpose of these exercises is to cultivate concentrated attention, enabling you to control your mind and direct your thoughts just as effectively as you can control your physical actions.

Exercise 8

Concentration on Internal Sensations. Lie down and completely relax your muscles. Focus your attention on the rhythmic beating of your heart, disregarding all other distractions. Contemplate how this vital organ pumps blood to every part of your body, envisioning the blood flowing in a steady stream from the heart to the toes and fingertips. With practice, you may even begin to feel the blood coursing through your system.

If you experience weakness or fatigue in any part of your body, visualize an increased flow of blood to that area. For example, if your eyes feel tired, imagine the blood traveling from the heart, up through the head, and out to the eyes. This exercise can significantly enhance your strength and vitality. Some individuals have developed such mastery over their heartbeats that they can temporarily halt them for several minutes, although this practice carries inherent risks and should not be attempted by beginners.

An additional exercise that can be beneficial before bedtime and upon waking is affirmations. Repeat to yourself, "Every cell in my body thrives with vitality; every part of my body is robust and healthy." Many people have reported significant improvements in their health by consistently reinforcing positive affirmations. Remember, you become what you envision yourself to be. If you focus on thoughts of illness, you may manifest sickness, but if you visualize yourself as strong and healthy, you will embody that image and experience vibrant health.

Exercise 9

Concentration on Sleep Induction. The "water method" is a simple yet effective technique for promoting sleep. Place a full glass of clear water on a table in your bedroom. Sit in a chair next to the table and gaze into the glass, contemplating its calmness. Visualize yourself entering a similarly tranquil state. Soon, you'll notice your nerves quieting, facilitating the transition into sleep. Alternatively, you can imagine yourself becoming drowsy to encourage sleepiness. Some individuals with persistent insomnia have found relief by envisioning themselves as inanimate objects, such as a hollow log in a serene forest.

Those struggling with insomnia will find these relaxation exercises invaluable for calming their nerves and promoting restful sleep. Maintain the belief that falling asleep is effortless, banishing any fear of insomnia. With consistent practice, you will establish healthier sleep patterns and enjoy rejuvenating rest.

By now, you should recognize the profound impact of concentration and its significance in enhancing various aspects of your life.

Exercise 10

Concentration for Energy Conservation and Appearance Enhancement. Observe yourself closely and notice if you have any habits of fidgeting with your hands, tapping your fingers, or twirling your mustache. Some individuals may unconsciously keep their feet in motion, such as tapping them on the floor. Stand before a mirror and assess whether you tend to frown or create wrinkles on your forehead. Also, observe others and note any unnecessary facial movements or expressions during conversation. Any facial movements that cause skin wrinkling can eventually lead to permanent wrinkles. Like a piece of silk, the face can withstand occasional folding and smooth out naturally, but repeated folding will result in permanent creases.

Through concentration, you can overcome the habit of worrying excessively. Take a few moments to focus on how trivial and unnecessary worrying is. If you find yourself becoming irritable or nervous over minor matters, immediately intervene and check your reaction. Take deep breaths, affirm to yourself, "I refuse to succumb to weakness; I am in control of myself," and you will swiftly regain composure.

Exercise 11

Controlling Temper through Concentration. If you're someone who easily loses their temper at the slightest provocation without attempting to control yourself, take a moment to reflect on its consequences. Does it serve any purpose? Does it disrupt your composure for some time? Are you aware that this behavior can lead to others despising you? Instead of reacting angrily to mistakes made by others, offer constructive feedback such as, "Please be more careful next time." This approach leaves a positive impression and encourages improvement. Conversely, constantly complaining about mistakes reinforces the idea of failure, increasing the likelihood of future errors. By learning to concentrate, you can overcome any lack of self-control.

Some of you may believe you're not guilty of these faults, but upon close observation, you may realize otherwise. If so, repeating the following affirmation each morning can be beneficial: "Today, I will avoid unnecessary gestures, worry over trifles, and refrain from becoming nervous or irritable. I am committed to remaining calm, regardless of circumstances, and exercising self-control. I resolve to eliminate all signs of lack of self-control from my behavior." Reflect on your actions at night to assess your adherence to this affirmation. Initially, you may falter, but persist, and you'll soon embody self-control. Once attained, maintain it by reaffirming your commitment in the morning and evaluating your conduct in the evening. Over time, self-control will become second nature.

Many individuals have attested to the transformative impact of this affirmation and daily review on their lives. You too will notice significant changes if you adhere to these instructions.

Exercise 12

Practicing Effective Communication Before a Mirror. Mark two points on your mirror at eye level and visualize them as human eyes gazing into yours. Initially, you may experience slight blinking, but focus on keeping your head perfectly still while standing upright. Concentrate solely on maintaining stillness, without allowing any other thoughts to intrude. Then, envision yourself appearing trustworthy and dependable—someone whom others would instinctively trust. Avoid behaviors that might elicit negative judgments about your trustworthiness.

While standing before the mirror, practice deep breathing and ensure the room is filled with fresh air. As the air permeates every cell of your body, feelings of timidity will dissipate, replaced by a sense of tranquility and strength. Individuals who exhibit control over their facial muscles and posture naturally command attention and make a stronger impression in conversations. They exude a sense of calmness and authority that can dissolve opposition effortlessly.

Exercise 13

Control of Sensations. Imagine how you would feel if you were cool, then how you would feel if you were cold, and finally, how you would feel if it were freezing—imagine shivering all over. Now reverse these conditions; vividly imagine heat until you can experience the sensation even in cold surroundings. With practice, you can train your imagination to achieve this, making undesirable conditions more tolerable.

Similarly, when experiencing hunger or thirst but unable to eat or drink, visualize yourself finishing a hearty meal instead of dwelling on your hunger or thirst. Likewise, when in pain, divert your attention instead of focusing on the pain, and you'll find it becomes more manageable. By systematically practicing such techniques, you'll gain remarkable control over factors affecting your physical comfort.

Exercise 14

Eastern Concentration Technique. Sit upright in a chair with a high back. Close one nostril with a finger and take a slow, deep breath, counting to ten as you inhale. Then exhale through the same nostril, counting to ten again. Repeat this process with the other nostril. Perform this exercise at least twenty times during each session.

Exercise 15

Controlling Desires. Desire, a challenging force to control, provides excellent concentration exercises. Although it may feel natural to share what you know, resisting this impulse strengthens your concentration. Focus on attending to your own affairs instead of gossiping about others.

If you learn something detrimental about someone, refrain from sharing it, as your opinion may be inaccurate, and withholding it reinforces your willpower. Similarly, when you hear good news, resist the urge to immediately share it. Mastering this control over desires prevents unnecessary trouble for both yourself and others. Once you have full control over your desires, you can share news confidently. Those lacking this control often divulge information unnecessarily, causing unnecessary complications.

Exercise 16

When You Read. Clear thinking requires concentration. Every individual should train themselves to think clearly. An effective exercise is to read a short story and then write a condensed summary. Attempt to express the essentials of a newspaper article in as few words as possible. Reading with the intent to extract only essential information demands intense concentration. If you struggle to articulate what you've read, it indicates a weakness in concentration. Alternatively, orally express the main points as if explaining to someone else. Such exercises are invaluable for developing concentration and enhancing thinking abilities.

After practicing these exercises, read a book for twenty minutes and then summarize what you've read. Initially, you may recall few details, but with practice, you'll improve. The more focused your concentration, the more accurate your account will be.

Another useful practice, especially when time is limited, is to read a short sentence and then attempt to write it verbatim. Gradually increase the number of sentences and continue until the habit is established. Consistent practice of these exercises enhances concentration remarkably. To remember every word in a sentence, you must exclude all other thoughts, a skill that alone justifies the effort of the exercise. Success in these exercises relies heavily on developing the ability to visualize or picture what you read.

Exercise 17

Concentration Overcomes Bad Habits. To overcome a habit, visualize your true self standing before you with your eyes closed.

Employ the power of affirmation; tell yourself, "You are not weak; you can break this habit. It's detrimental, and you want to overcome it." Imagine yourself as another person offering this advice. This practice allows you to see yourself objectively, weakening the grip of the habit and granting you freedom.

By forming a mental image of controlling yourself as another person might, you'll find pleasure in breaking bad habits. Many individuals have successfully overcome habits, such as drinking, using this method.

Exercise 18

Clock Concentration. Sit in a chair and place a clock with a second hand on the table. Focus your eyes on the second hand as it moves around the clock face for five minutes. During this time, think only about the second hand, keeping all other thoughts subordinate to it. Although the second hand may not be particularly captivating, the effort of willpower required to maintain focus on it adds value to the exercise. Endeavor to remain as still as possible during this practice, as it helps in gaining control over nerves and promotes a calming effect on them.

Exercise 19

Faith Concentration. Belief in the power of concentration is crucial. This exercise is intentionally placed here to emphasize that you can indeed learn to concentrate. If you have practiced the previous exercises, you've likely developed considerable concentration power, instilling faith in its effectiveness. However, you can further strengthen your belief in it.

If you have a desire or wish to be fulfilled, or seek special advice, first clearly visualize what you want and then concentrate on attaining it. Have absolute faith that your desires will manifest. Believe unwaveringly in their fulfillment. Do not dwell on why or how it will happen; simply focus on achieving what you desire, and it will be yours.

A Caution. Never entertain thoughts of failure; instead, envision your desired outcome as already accomplished, and it will manifest.

Overcoming Self-Distrust. Do you sometimes doubt yourself? If so, inquire which aspect of yourself you mistrust. Remind yourself that your higher self remains unaffected by doubts. Reflect on the extraordinary powers of your higher self. There exists a solution to every difficulty, and it is gratifying for the human spirit to overcome challenges.

Rather than expending energy dreading or fearing unpleasant situations, redirect your thoughts towards making the best of them. Most of our troubles are mere fabrications of the mind, and the habit of dreading them only serves to attract more negativity. Your circumstances are influenced by your negative thoughts and fears, but you possess the inherent ability to triumph over them.

To combat self-doubt, contemplate why you are concentrating your efforts. By doing so, you establish a stronger connection with your higher self, which remains unwavering in its trust.

Lesson 15

Concentrate so You will not Forget

A man forgets because he fails to concentrate his mind on his purpose, especially at the moment of conceiving it. We recall only what leaves a deep impression, so we must initially deepen our impressions by associating certain ideas related to them in our minds.

For instance, consider a wife giving her husband a letter to mail. If he merely puts it in his pocket without thoughtful consideration, he may forget about it altogether. However, if, at the moment the letter is handed to him, he consciously says to himself, "I will mail this letter. The mailbox is at the next corner, and when I pass it, I must drop this letter," it would enable him to remember the task as soon as he reaches the mailbox.

The same principle applies to more significant tasks. Suppose you're instructed to visit Mr. Smith during your lunch break today. You are less likely to forget if, at the time of receiving the instruction, you say something like, "When I get to the corner of Blank street on my way to lunch, I shall turn right and call on Mr. Smith." This way, the impression is strengthened, the connection is established, and seeing the associated object triggers the memory of the errand.

The crucial step is to deepen the impression the moment it enters your mind. This is achieved not only by focusing your mind on the idea itself but also by surrounding it with associations so that each idea reinforces the others.

The mind operates on the laws of association, where ideas that enter the mind simultaneously tend to emerge simultaneously, aiding in recalling one another. The reason people struggle to remember what they want is that they haven't sufficiently concentrated their minds on their purpose when it was formed.

You can train your memory by concentrating your attention on your purpose, following the laws of association. Once this habit is formed, attention becomes easily centered, and memory is effectively trained. Instead of failing at crucial moments, your memory becomes a valuable asset in your everyday work.

Memory Concentration Exercise: Choose a picture, place it on a table, and gaze at it for two minutes. Concentrate on every detail, then close your eyes and recall as much as you can about it. Consider the subject, its natural appearance, foreground, middle ground, background, color, and form details. Open your eyes, correct any mistakes, and repeat until your mental image matches the original.

Nature is a Wonderful Instructor, but few realize that connecting with nature helps us discover ourselves. By listening to her voice with our inner sense, we learn the unity of life and awaken our latent powers.

Few people realize that the simple act of listening and concentrating is our most potent inner power, as it brings us into close contact with the highest, just as our other senses connect us with the coarser side of human nature. The closer we live to nature, the more developed this sense becomes. The so-called civilization has overdeveloped our other senses at the expense of this one.

Children instinctively grasp the value of concentration. For example, when a child encounters a challenging problem and reaches a difficult point mentally, despite earnest efforts, they will pause and remain still, seemingly listening. If you observe closely, you'll witness a sudden illumination, and the child proceeds happily to accomplish the task. A child, instinctively and unconsciously, knows that when help is needed, quietness and concentration are essential.

All accomplished individuals practice concentration and attribute their success to it. A doctor reflects on the symptoms of a patient, patiently waits, and listens for inspiration, even if unaware of doing so. One who diagnoses in this manner seldom makes mistakes. An author contemplates the plot, holds it in their mind, waits, and experiences illumination. To solve intricate problems effectively, you must learn to do the same.

Lesson 16

How Concentration can Fulfill Your Sesire

"It is a spiritual law that the desire to do necessarily implies the ability to do."

You have all come across the tale of "Aladdin's Lamp," which performed extraordinary feats. While this is a mere fairy story, it serves to illustrate that within man lies the power, if harnessed effectively, to fulfill every wish.

If you find yourself unable to satisfy your deepest longings, it is high time you discover how to utilize your God-given powers. Soon, you will become aware of latent abilities within you that, once developed, can unveil priceless knowledge and boundless possibilities for success.

Man deserves abundance in all aspects, not merely sustenance, as so many settle for. All natural desires are achievable. It would be unjust for the Infinite to create needs that cannot be met. The essence of all created things lies in man's power to think, and thus, every instinct leads to thought. In every thought resides great potential, as true thought development, coupled with mysterious powers that may transcend it, has propelled the world's genuine progress.

In moments of silence, we become conscious of "that something" beyond thought, utilizing thought as a medium for expression. While many catch glimpses of "that something," few reach the state where the mind is steady enough to fathom these depths. Silent, concentrated thought holds greater potency than spoken words, as speech diverts the mind's focus by drawing more attention to the external.

Man must increasingly learn to rely on himself, seeking the Infinite within. It is from this source alone that he gains the power to solve practical difficulties. Never should one give up, for the resources of Infinity are ever-present. The root of failure lies in searching in the wrong direction for success, oblivious to the real powers within that, when activated, can guide them.

The Infinite within remains elusive to those who journey through life without developing their spiritual powers. The Infinite aids only those who help themselves. There is no concept of a special "Providence." Assistance from the Infinite comes only to the extent that one believes, hopes, and prays for help from this tremendous source.

Concentrate on What You Want and Get It. The weakling is controlled by conditions; the strong man controls conditions. You can be either the conqueror or the conquered. Through the law of concentration, you can attain your heart's desire. This law is so potent that what initially appears impossible becomes achievable.

By this law, what you initially perceive as a dream transforms into reality.

Remember, the first step in concentration is to create a mental image of what you wish to accomplish. This image becomes a thought-seed that attracts thoughts of a similar nature. Around this thought, once planted in the imagination or creative region of the mind, you build associated thoughts that continue to grow as long as your desire compels close concentration.

Cultivate the habit of focusing on something you wish to accomplish for five minutes each day. Exclude all other thoughts from consciousness. Be confident in your success; determine that all obstacles in your way will be overcome, enabling you to rise above any environment.

Achieve this by harnessing the natural laws of the thought world, which are immensely powerful.

A valuable aid in concentration development is to write out your thoughts on what lies closest to your heart. Gradually add to it until you have exhausted the subject as much as possible. Each day, as you concentrate your forces on this thought at the center of the stream of consciousness, new plans, ideas, and methods will flash into your mind. There is a law of attraction that will assist you in achieving your purpose.

Consider an advertiser, for instance, thinking along a certain line. Although he has formed his ideas, he seeks others' perspectives. Starting the search, he discovers numerous books, plans, designs, etc., on the subject, initially unaware of their existence.

This principle holds true in all fields. We can attract what aids us. Often, help seems to arrive miraculously. It may be gradual, but once the silent unseen forces are activated, they bring results as long as we play our part. Always present and ready to assist those who choose to use them, these forces operate when you form a strong mental image of your desire, planting the thought-seed that works in your favor, ultimately materializing if in harmony with your higher nature.

It may appear unnecessary to remind you to concentrate only on achievements that benefit you without causing harm to others, but many, in their eagerness for success, forget the rights of fellow travelers on life's road. All good things are within your reach, provided you align your forces with the law demanding justice toward others. Reflect on your desired goal, assessing whether it is beneficial for you, and affirm, "I want to achieve this; I will work to attain it. The way will open for me."

By mentally embracing the thought of success daily, you gradually create a pattern or mold that will materialize over time.

Crucially, avoid doubt and fear, the destructive forces. Never let them associate with your thoughts.

Eventually, you will shape the desired conditions and receive unexpected help that elevates you from an undesirable environment. Life will then take on a different hue as you discover happiness through awakening the power to master circumstances, not be enslaved by them.

To those new to this line of thought, some statements in this book may sound strange or even absurd. Instead of dismissing them, give them a try—they will prove effective.

Consider the inventor who mentally develops an idea before materializing it. The architect envisions the house mentally before planning and building it. Every object, every venture, originates as a mental creation.

I know a man who began with thirteen cents and no credit. In a decade, he built a large, profitable business. His success, he attributes to two things: belief in his success and hard work. Despite facing storms and creditor pressure, he maintained a bold front, securing extensions when needed. When required to raise a specific sum at a particular time, he always did. By concentrating on the belief that certain individuals owed him and would pay by a set date, he consistently received their checks, often at the last mail of the extension day. His unwavering belief in the power of affecting others' minds through concentration rarely left him disappointed.

Exert the required concentrated effort, and you will receive wonderful assistance from sources unknown to you. Recall the profound words of Jesus, the Master: "Whatever you desire, when you pray, pray as if you had already received, and you shall have."

Lesson 17

Deals Developed by Concentration

Through our paltry stir and strife, Glows the wished Ideal, and longing molds in clay, what life Carves in the marble real. – Lowell.

People are often referred to as idealists, and the truth is, we are all idealists to some degree. Our ultimate success depends on the ideals we envision. A mental image is essential to produce a material thing; everything is first created in the mind. When you control your thoughts, you become a creator, shaping divine ideas to meet your individual needs. Your perspective determines the nature of all things in your world. Happiness and success hinge on your ideals.

You are accountable for every condition you experience, whether consciously or unconsciously. The next step you take determines the subsequent one. Concentrate on each step along the way to save unnecessary steps, choosing a direct path rather than a circuitous route. Concentrate on your ideals, and they will manifest in tangible realities. Through concentration, we bring our ideals into physical existence. Your future relies on the ideals you are currently forming, with past ideals determining your present. To secure a bright future, start preparing today.

If people realized that by seemingly harming others, they are ultimately injuring themselves, the world would be vastly different. A person's changeability is often attributed to shifting ideals. Every alteration in your ideal prompts a shift in thinking, leaving you like a rudderless boat on the ocean. Understand the importance of holding onto your ideal until it materializes into reality.

Consider waking up determined not to lose your temper. This idealizes a person of strength and poise. Yet, when something upsets you, and you lose your temper, you momentarily forget your ideal. Reflecting on what a well-poised person implies could prevent anger. Losing poise occurs when ideals are forgotten. Each time ideals shatter, willpower weakens. Holding onto ideals develops willpower—do not forget this.

Why do many men fail? Because they fail to cling to their ideal until it becomes a mental habit. When they concentrate solely on it, excluding all else, it transforms into reality."I am that which I think myself to be."

Ideals are reflected to us from the unseen spirit. The laws of matter and spirit are not the same. One can be broken, but not the other. The extent to which ideals are upheld assures your future.

It was never intended for man to suffer; he has brought it upon himself by disobeying the laws of nature. He is aware of these laws, so ignorance cannot be pleaded. Why does he break them? Because he does not pay attention to those ideals flashed to him from the Infinite Spirit.

Life is one continuous unfoldment, and you can be happy every step of the way or miserable, as you please. It all depends on how we entertain those silent whisperings that come from we know not where. We cannot hear them with mortal ears, but from the silence, they come as if they were dreams, not to you or me alone, but to everyone. In this way, the grandest thoughts come to us, to use or abuse. So, search not in treasured volumes for noble thoughts, but within, and a bright and glowing vision will come to be realized now and hereafter.

You must dedicate some hours to concentrated, consistent, persistent thought. You must study yourself and your weaknesses. No man gets over a fence by wishing himself on the other side. He must climb. Similarly, no man gets out of the rut of dull, tiresome, monotonous life by merely wishing himself out of the rut. He must climb.

If you are standing still or going backward, there is something wrong. You are the person to find out what is wrong. Don't think that you are neglected, not understood, or not appreciated. Such thoughts are the thoughts of failure. Consider that men who have achieved what you envy got it by working for it. Don't pity yourself; criticize yourself. You know that the only thing in the world that you have to count upon is yourself.

Lesson 18

Mental Control through Creation

I recently attended a banquet of inventors where each innovator shared thoughts on future accomplishments. Many much-needed ideas were discussed. One inventor particularly emphasized the possibilities of wireless telephones, predicting the imminent annihilation of distance. He envisioned a future where we could communicate with someone in a submarine forty fathoms below the surface and a thousand miles away. After his talk, he asked if anyone doubted his vision. No one spoke up, not out of tactful politeness but because no one present truly doubted that the inventor's vision would materialize in the future.

These astute individuals, some genuine geniuses, foresaw a time when we could talk to those a thousand miles away without any medium. If we can create an instrument that allows us to send wireless messages over a thousand miles, is there any reason why we cannot, through mental control, transmit messages from one person to another? The transmission of a wireless message should not be easier than projecting a thought.

A day will come when all businesses will employ highly developed individuals to emit influential forces. These influences will be so commanding that employees will be partly controlled by them, allowing you to profit more from your mental powers. You will consistently send suggestions to your employees and friends. They will receive these unconsciously, but if your personality is stronger, they will act on them as if you had spoken them.

This practice is already in motion today. A well-organized company harnesses the combined effort of all its employees. They may each be engaged in different kinds of work, but collectively, they strive to achieve the best results. The entire atmosphere is permeated with a high standard of workmanship, compelling everyone to do their best in such surroundings.

A business will succeed only to the extent that the efforts of all are coordinated towards one result. At least one person is needed to direct everyone toward the desired end. The person at the helm doesn't have to precisely outline the steps to others, but they must possess the mental power to control others.

An up-to-date business letter is not written casually or in a commonplace way today. The writer strives to convey something interesting to the receiver, awakening a responsive spirit. Sometimes, the addition of a word or two can transform a matter-of-fact letter into one that compels a response. It's not always the content of a letter but the spirit it breathes that brings results. The intangible something that defies analysis is the projected thought of the master that brings back the harvest it claims.

We should not solely claim success for ourselves. If you desire a friend or relative to succeed, envision them achieving success. Picture them in the position you'd like to see them in. If there are weaknesses, command them to be strengthened. Think of their negative aspects being replaced by positive qualities. Dedicate a part of your day to sending thoughts of encouragement. This can activate their mental powers, and once activated, they will assert themselves and achieve their potential.

We have the capacity to accomplish more than we often believe by sending direct, positive, and controlling suggestions of leadership to others. However, a person's success is greatly determined by how they act on the received suggestions.

Life is a continuous cycle of advancement or decline; there's no standing still. Each accomplishment builds the ability to achieve greater things. As a business grows, so must its leader. The head of a business needs to advance and serve as a guiding influence. By their power to control, they inspire confidence in those around them. Employees may possess superior qualities, and with proper development, they could become influential employers themselves.

Through your mental power, you can instill enthusiasm and a spirit of success in others, providing the impetus to pursue worthwhile endeavors.

In concentrated mental control, there's a latent power more potent than physical force. The person realizes that the mind's attitude can control, direct, and govern other forces, enabling them to acquire what they desire.

Regardless of strength, everyone is affected by the mental forces in their environment. No one can remain neutral to influences. The mind is not immune to the forces of a place. If your business environment is not helpful, it will be harmful, highlighting the importance of a positive workplace. Changing positions can often be beneficial.

No one was intended to live alone. Solitary confinement leads to mental starvation, narrowing the mind and weakening mental powers. Living alone can contribute to mild forms of insanity. Association with peers is vital for mental well-being. Children playing with their own age group develop accordingly, and the same applies to older individuals associating with younger people. Like attracts like worldwide.

The thought element plays a significant role in our lives. In any business, it is not only physical effort that needs to be commanded but also thought effort. There must be coordination of thought, and employers should aim to secure employees who think along similar lines. This shared mindset fosters fuller sympathy, better understanding, and mutual assistance among team members. It contributes to the creation of a perfect organization where each individual, like a spoke in a big wheel, carries their load without shirking. Working in such an atmosphere encourages individuals to produce their best work.

Great leaders must be able to inspire a cooperative spirit. They achieve this through mental control, making their assistants realize the value of such control. A close bond is formed, and the team works toward a single purpose, profiting from their combined effort to accomplish much.

In a business conducted with the right spirit, the leader can instill their thoughts and ideas into employees. Unbeknownst to them, the leader's mental forces shape their work, ensuring results just as physical forces in nature do.

The modern businessperson of the future will prioritize getting employees to think and reason better, avoiding depression or discouragement. Instead of wasting time, efforts will be directed towards concentrated efforts that benefit both employer and employee. The spirit of justice must play a more significant role in the businesses of the future.

I know of a firm that will not hire an employee until they have filled out an application blank. While applicants may think it is a trivial process, a capable manager can assess, through the application, whether the person will fit into the management structure.

The primary concern for the manager is to gauge the applicant's capacity for efficient cooperative effort. They seek individuals who have faith in themselves and are aware that discussing misfortunes and feeling blue may communicate a depressing influence to others. The modern manager aims to avoid hiring employees who could hinder the success of the team.

It is crucial to recognize that every moment spent dwelling on past difficulties or in bad company attracts negative influences.

Overcoming these influences is necessary for personal advancement.

Some firms prefer hiring individuals with no prior work experience, as they have nothing to unlearn and are more easily guided. These newcomers, lacking bad business habits, quickly grasp new methods, receive mental support from the management, and become efficient and skilled workers.

Many large business firms today employ efficiency experts who, through their training and experience, introduce individuals with little business experience to refined plans. The right attitude plays a significant role in success, and we must learn to generate helpful forces through the controlled and projected power of our thoughts. Developing this power through concentration is crucial for maximizing its potential.

We find ourselves surrounded by numerous forces, many of which are currently beyond our understanding. Our awareness of these forces is destined to expand significantly. With each passing year, our understanding of psychic forces grows, revealing vast possibilities of which we are only faintly aware. To harness these higher powers and forces that will undoubtedly shape the destinies of countless future generations, it is essential to believe in, explore, and utilize mental control.

Lesson 19

Concentrated will Development

New Method: In this chapter, you will discover a highly effective and practical approach to cultivating your willpower. With dedication, you can transform your will into a powerful force capable of attracting immense strength. The exercises provided are designed to strengthen your will, similar to how you would enhance your muscles through athletic training.

Every endeavor begins with foundational principles, and simple exercises will be introduced. The potential benefits of mental cultivation through concentration exercises are immeasurable. Even the seemingly basic exercises hold value. As Dr. Oppenheim notes, "In no respect can a man show a finer quality of will-power than in his own private, intimate life." Our will determines our capacity for justice, purity of thought, charitable opinions, and forbearance in overlooking others' shortcomings—all aspects controlled by the will. Therefore, integrating will-training exercises into our daily lives is essential.

Recognizing the need to train your will is crucial, and you must understand that this effort demands self-command, which only you can provide. While I can guide you in the process, your success hinges on your mastery and consistent application of these methods.

New Methods of Will-Training: Begin by selecting a quiet, uninterrupted room. Equip yourself with a watch to track time and a notebook to record observations. Start each exercise by noting the date and time of day.

Exercise 1

Choose a convenient time of the day. Sit in a chair and focus on the door-knob for ten minutes. Then, document your experiences. Initially, it may feel strange and unnatural, and holding one position for ten minutes could be challenging. However, strive to remain as still as possible. The duration might seem lengthy, especially if it's the first time you've sat doing nothing for ten minutes. Your thoughts may wander from the door-knob, and you may question the purpose of this exercise. Repeat it for six days.

10 P. M. 2nd Day.

Notes: You should be able to sit more quietly, and time should pass more swiftly. You might feel a bit stronger due to improved will control. Keeping this resolution will uplift and brace you.

10 P. M. 3rd Day.

Notes: Concentrating on the door-knob may be harder, especially after a busy day. Persist, banish foreign thoughts, and desire more control. Achieving this control instills a powerful feeling, making you feel more significant, noble, and manly. You'll acknowledge, "I can actually do what I want and dispel foreign thoughts. The exercise is valuable."

10 P. M. 4th Day.

Notes: Instantly concentrating on the door-knob becomes easier. Overcoming leg movement and establishing self-directed focus demonstrate mental strength. Recognizing the value of mastering your will-force, you gain self-confidence and feel increased self-control.

10 P. M. 5th Day.

Notes: Concentration intensifies daily, and you feel capable of focusing on anything you wish.

10 P. M. 6th Day.

Notes: Instantly centering your attention on the door-knob indicates thorough mastery of the exercise, preparing you for the next challenge.

Having completed this exercise, write a summary of your success in controlling fleeting impulses of the mind and will. This practice is excellent, offering valuable insights into the mind's wonderful and subtle activities.

Exercise 2

Acquire a deck of playing cards. Choose a specific time for the exercise. Each day, at the designated time, take the pack in one hand and start laying the cards down on top of each other as slowly and evenly as possible. Ensure each card completely covers the one beneath. Continue this exercise for six days.

1st Day.

Notes: The task feels tedious and tiresome, demanding close concentration to achieve even coverage. There might be a temptation to lay the cards down faster, but it's crucial to maintain a slow pace. Patience is required, and the exercise exposes impulsive tendencies. Practicing this calm approach enhances control over hands and arms, fostering a newfound calmness. You recognize the impulsive nature and how willpower can temper your temperament.

2nd Day.

Notes: Initially, laying the cards down slowly requires effort, but practice allows for increased speed. The challenge is to resist the urge to hurry. The slow, steady movement proves wearisome, necessitating conquering the desire to rush. Eventually, mastery allows you to control the pace at will.

3rd Day.

Notes: Going slowly remains challenging, especially for impulsive individuals. This exercise is mentally bracing, as it involves concentrating on disagreeable tasks. It becomes a lesson in overcoming impulsiveness. Documenting these notes proves helpful.

4th Day.

Notes: The realization of placing cards mathematically surfaces. Carelessness emerges, prompting the command to concentrate more. Bringing the will under control seems less difficult, and the exercise becomes an avenue for gaining more poise.

5th Day.

Notes: Jerky movements are overcome, enabling the slow and steady laying of cards. A sense of rapidly gaining poise emerges, emphasizing better control over the will. The will is recognized as a significant governing power, and the exercise is deemed valuable for accomplishing tasks.

6th Day.

Notes: The exercise reveals the wonderful possibilities of the will, emphasizing its potential impact.

It gives me strength to think of the power of will. I am able to do so much more and better work now, realizing that I can control my will's action. Whatever my task, my will is concentrated on it. I am to keep my will centered there until the task is finished. The more closely and definitely I determine what I shall do, the more easily the will carries it out. Determination imparts compelling force to the will. It exerts itself more. The will and the end act and react on each other.

7th Day.

Notes: Now try to do everything you do today faster. Don't hurry or become nervous. Just try to do everything faster but in a steady manner.

You will find that the exercises you have practiced in retardation have steadied your nerves, thereby making it possible to increase your speed. The will is under your command. Make it carry out resolutions rapidly. This is how you build up your self-control and your self-command. It is then that the human machine acts as its author dictates.

You certainly should now be able to judge the great benefit that comes from writing out your introspections each day. Of course, you will not have the exact experiences given in these examples, but some of these will fit your case. Be careful to study your experiences carefully and make as true a report as you can. Describe your feelings just as they seem to you. Allow your fancies to color your report, and it will be worthless. You have pictured conditions as you see them. In a few months, if you again try the same exercises, you will find your report very much better. By these introspections, we learn to know ourselves better and with this knowledge can wonderfully increase our efficiency. As you become used to writing out your report, it will be more accurate. You thus learn how to govern your impulses, activities, and weaknesses.

Each person should try to plan exercises that will best fit his needs. If not convenient for you to practice exercises every day, take them twice or three times a week. But carry out any plan you decide to try. If you cannot devote ten minutes a day to the experiments, start with five minutes and gradually increase the time. The exercises given are only intended for examples.

Will Training Without Exercise. Many people do not want to take the time to practice exercises, so the following instructions for training the will are given to them.

By willing and realizing, the will grows. Therefore, the more you will, the more it grows and builds up power. No matter whether your task is big or small, make it a rule to accomplish it to fortify your will. Form the habit of focusing your will in all its strength upon the subject to be achieved. You form in this way the habit of getting a thing done, of carrying out some plan. You acquire the feeling of being able to accomplish that which lies before you, no matter what it is. This gives you confidence and a sense of power that you get in no other way. You know when you make a resolution that you will keep it. You do not tackle new tasks in a half-hearted way but with a bold, brave spirit. We know that the will is able to carry us over big obstacles. Knowing this, despair never claims us for a victim. We have wills and are going to use them with more and more intensity, thus giving us the power to make our resolutions stronger, our actions freer, and our lives finer and better.

The education of the will should not be left to chance. It is only definite tasks that will render it energetic, ready, persevering, and consistent. The only way it can be done is by self-study and self-discipline. The cost is effort, time, and patience, but the returns are valuable. There are no magical processes leading to will development, but the development of your will works wonders for you because it gives you self-mastery, personal power, and energy of character.

Concentration of the Will to Win. The adaptability of persons to their business environment is more a matter of determination than anything else. In this age, we hear a good deal of talk about a man's aptitudes. Some of his aptitudes, some of his powers, may be developed to a wonderful extent, but he is really an unknown quantity until all his latent powers are developed to their highest possible extent. He may be a failure in one line and a big success in another. Many successful men did not succeed well at what they first undertook, but they profited by their efforts in different directions, and this fitted them for higher things. If they had refused to adjust themselves to their environment, the tide of progress would have swept them into oblivion.

My one aim in all my works is to try to arouse in the individual the effort and determination to develop his full capacities, his highest possibilities. One thing I want you to realize at the start is that it is not so much ability as it is the will to do that counts. Ability is very plentiful, but organizing initiative and creative power are not as common. It is easy to get employees, but to get someone to train them is harder. Their abilities must be directed to the work they can do. They must be shown how, while at this work, to conserve their energy, and they must be taught to work in harmony with others, for most business concerns are dominated by a single personality.

Concentrating on Driving Force Within. We are all conscious, at times, that we have somewhere within us an active driving force that is ever trying to push us onward to better deeds. It is that "force" that makes us feel determined at times to do something worthwhile. It is not thought, emotion, or feeling. This driving force is something distinct from thought or emotion. It is a quality of the soul, and therefore it has consciousness all its own. It is the "I will do" of the will. It is the force that makes the will concentrate. Many have felt this force working within them, driving them on to accomplish their tasks. All great men and women become conscious that this supreme and powerful force is their ally in carrying out great resolutions.

This driving force is within all, but until you reach a certain stage, you do not become aware of it. It is most useful to the worthy. It springs up naturally without any thought of training. It comes unprovoked and leaves unnoticed. Just what this force is, we do not know, but we do know that it is what intensifies the will in demanding just and harmonious action.

The ordinary human being, merely as merchandise, if he could be sold as a slave, would be worth ten thousand dollars. If somebody gave you a five thousand dollar automobile, you would take very good care of it. You wouldn't put sand in the carburetor, or mix water with the gasoline, or drive it furiously over rough roads, or leave it out to freeze at night.

Are you quite sure that you take care of your own body, your own health, your only real property, as well as you would take care of a five thousand dollar automobile if it were given to you?

The man who mixes whiskey with his blood is more foolish than a man would be if he mixed water with gasoline in his car. You can get another car; you cannot get another body. The man who misses sleep lives irregularly, bolting his food so that his blood supply is imperfect. That is a foolish man treating himself as he would not treat any other valuable piece of property.

Do you try to talk with men and women who know more than you do, and do you LISTEN rather than try to tell them what you know? There are a hundred thousand men of fifty and men of sixty running along in the old rut, any one of whom could get out of it and be counted among the successful men if only the spark could be found to explode the energy within them now going to waste. Each man must study and solve his own problem.

Lesson 20

Concentration Reviewed

In bringing this book to a close, I again want to impress upon you the inestimable value of concentration. Those who lack this great power or fail to develop it will generally suffer from poverty and unhappiness, and their life's work will most often be a failure. Meanwhile, those who develop and use it will make the most of life's opportunities.

I have tried to make these lessons practical, and I am sure that many will find them so. Of course, the mere reading of them will not do you a great deal of good, but if the exercises are practiced, worked out, and applied to your own individual case, you should be able to acquire the habit of concentration to such a measure as to greatly improve your work and increase your happiness.

Remember, the best instruction can only help you to the extent to which you put it into practice. I have found it an excellent idea to read a book through first, then re-read it. When you come to an idea that appeals to you, stop and think about it. If applicable to you, repeat it over and over so that you will be impressed by it. In this way, you can form the habit of picking out all the good things you read, and these will have a wonderful influence on your character.

In this closing chapter, I want to impress upon you to concentrate on what you do, instead of performing most of your work unconsciously or automatically, until you have formed habits that give you mastery of your work and your life powers and forces.

Very often, the hardest part of work is thinking about it. When you get right into it, it does not seem so disagreeable. This is the experience of many when they first commence to learn how to concentrate. So never think it a difficult task, but undertake it with the "I Will Spirit," and you will find that its acquisition will be as easy as its application will be useful.

Read the life of any great man, and you will generally find that the dominant quality that made him successful was the ability to concentrate. Study those that have been failures, and you will often find that a lack of concentration was the cause.

"One thing at a time, and that done well is a good rule, as I can tell."

All men are not born with equal powers, but it is the way they are used that counts. "Opportunity knocks at every man's door." Those who are successful hear the knock and grasp the chance. The failures believe that luck and circumstances are against them. They always blame someone else instead of themselves for their lack of success. We get what is coming to us, nothing more or less. Anything within the universe is within your grasp. Just use your latent powers, and it is yours. You are aided by both visible and invisible forces when you concentrate on either "to do" or "to be."

Everyone is capable of some concentration, for without it, you would be unable to say or do anything. People differ in the power to concentrate because some are unable to will to hold the thought in mind for the required time. The amount of determination used determines who has the strongest will. No one's is stronger than yours. Think of this whenever you go against a strong opponent.

Never say "I can't concentrate today." You can do it just the minute you say "I will." You can keep your thoughts from straying, just the same as you can control your arms. When once you realize this fact, you can train the will to concentrate on anything you wish. If it wanders, it is your fault. You are not utilizing your will. But, don't blame it on your will and say it is weak. The will is just the same whether you act as if it were weak or as if it were strong. When you act as if your will is strong, you say, "I can." When you act as if it were weak, you say, "I can't." It requires the same amount of effort in each case.

Some men get in the habit of thinking "I can't" and they fail. Others think "I can" and succeed. So remember, it is for you to decide whether you will join the army of "I can't" or "I can."

The big mistake with so many is that they don't realize that when they say "I can't," they are really saying, "I won't try." You cannot tell what you can do until you try. "Can't" means you will not try. Never say you cannot concentrate, for when you do, you are really saying that you refuse to try.

Whenever you feel like saying, "I can't," say instead, "I possess all will and I can use as much as I wish." You only use as much as you have trained yourself to use.

An Experiment to Try: Before going to bed tonight, repeat, "I am going to choose my own thoughts and hold them as long as I choose. I am going to shut out all thoughts that weaken or interfere, that make me timid. My will is as strong as anyone else's. While going to work the next morning, repeat this over. Keep this up for a month, and you will find you will have a better opinion of yourself. These are the factors that make you a success. Hold fast to them always.

Concentration is nothing but willing to do a certain thing. All foreign thoughts can be kept out by willing that they stay out. You cannot realize your possibilities until you commence to direct your mind. You then do consciously what you have before done unconsciously. In this way, you note mistakes, overcome bad habits, and perfect your conduct.

At times, you have been in a position that required courage, and you were surprised at the amount you showed. Now, when once you arouse yourself, you have this courage all the time, and it is not necessary to have a special occasion reveal it to you. My object in so strongly impressing this on your mind is to make you aware that the same courage, the same determination that you show at certain exceptional times, you have at your command at all times. It is a part of your vast resources. Use it often and well, in working out the highest destiny of which you are capable.

Final Concentration Instruction: You now realize that, in order to make your life worthy, useful, and happy, you must concentrate. A number of exercises and all the needed instruction have been given. It now remains for you to form the highest ideal that you can in the present and live up to that ideal, and try to raise it. Don't waste your time in foolish reading. Select something that is inspiring, that you may become en rapport with those that think thoughts that are worth while. Their enthusiasm will inspire and enlighten you. Read slowly and concentrate on what you are reading. Let your spirit and the spirit of the author commune, and you will then sense what is between the lines—those great things which words cannot express.

Pay constant attention to one and one thing only for a given time, and you will soon be able to concentrate. Hang on to that thought ceaselessly until you have attained your object. When you work, let your mind dwell steadily on your task. Think before you speak and direct your conversation to the subject under discussion. Do not ramble. Talk slowly, steadily, and connectedly. Never form the hurry habit, but be deliberate in all you do. Assume static attitudes without moving a finger or an eyelid, or any part of your body. Read books that treat of but one continuous subject. Read long articles and recall the thread of the argument.

Associate yourself with people who are steady, patient, and tireless in their thought, action, and work. See how long you can sit still and think on one subject without interruption.

Concentrating on the Higher Self: Father Time keeps going on and on. Every day he rolls around means one less day for you on this planet. Most of us only try to master the external conditions of this world. We think our success and happiness depend on us doing so. These are, of course, important, and I don't want you to think they are not. But I want you to realize that when death comes, only those inherent and acquired qualities and conditions within the mentality—your character, conduct, and soul growth—will go with you. If these are what they should be, you need not be afraid of not being successful and happy, for with these qualities, you can mold external materials and conditions.

Study yourself. Find Your Strong Points and Make Them Stronger As Well As Your Weak Ones And Strengthen Them. Study yourself carefully, and you will see yourself as you really are. The secret of accomplishment is concentration or the art of turning all your power upon just one point at a time. If you have studied yourself carefully, you should have a good line on yourself and should be able to make the proper interior re-adjustments. Remember first, last, and always, Right thinking and right Living necessarily results in happiness, and it is therefore within your power to obtain happiness. Anyone that is not happy does not claim their birthright.

Keep in mind that someday you are going to leave this world and think of what you will take with you. This will assist you in concentrating on the higher forces. Now start from this minute to act according to the advice of the higher self in everything you do. If you do, its ever-harmonious forces will necessarily ensure you a successful fulfillment of all your life purposes.

Whenever you feel tempted to disobey your higher promptings, hold the thought "My-higher-self-insures-to-me-the-happiness-of-doing-that-which-best-answers-my-true-relations-to-all-others."

You possess latent talents that, when developed and utilized, are of assistance to you and others. But if you do not properly use them, you shirk your duty, and you will be the loser and suffer from the consequences. Others will also be worse off if you do not fulfill your obligations.

When you have aroused into activity your thought powers, you will realize the wonderful value of these principles in helping you to carry out your plans. The right, in the end, must prevail. You can assist in the working out of the great plan of the universe and thereby gain the reward, or you can work against the great plan and suffer the consequences. The all-consuming fires are gradually purifying all discordant elements. If you choose to work contrary to the law, you will burn in its crucible, so I want you to learn to concentrate intelligently on becoming in harmony with your higher self.

Hold the thought: "I-will-live-for-my-best. I-seek-wisdom, self-knowledge, happiness-and-power-to-help-others. I-act-from-the-higher-self, therefore-only-the-best-can-come-to-me." The more we become conscious of the presence of the higher self, the more we should try to become a true representative of the human soul in all its wholeness and holiness, instead of wasting our time dwelling on some trifling external quality or defect. We should try to secure a true conception of what we really are so as not to overvalue the external furnishings. You will then not surrender your dignity or self-respect when others ignorantly make a display of material things to show off. Only the person that realizes that he is a permanent Being knows what the true self is.